When to Say GOODBYE to Your THERAPIST

Catherine Johnson, Ph.D.

A Fireside Book
Published by Simon & Schuster Inc.
New York   London   Toronto   Sydney   Tokyo

Fireside
Simon & Schuster Building
Rockefeller Center
1230 Avenue of the Americas
New York, New York 10020

First Fireside Edition, 1989

FIRESIDE and colophon are registered trademarks
of Simon & Schuster Inc.

Designed by Irving Perkins Associates
Manufactured in the United States of America

10 9 8 7 6 5 4 3 2 1
10 9 8 7 6 5 4 3 2 1 Pbk.

Library of Congress Cataloging in Publication Data

Johnson, Catherine.
   When to say goodbye to your therapist.

    1. Psychotherapy—Termination.   2. Psychotherapist
and patient.   I. Title.
RC489.T45J63   1988   616.89′14   88-18453

ISBN 0-671-61888-1
ISBN 0-671-68846-4   Pbk.

This book is dedicated to my parents, Patricia and Robert Johnson, and to Ed, always.

CONTENTS

INTRODUCTION

Therapy has become routine. Nearly 40 percent of all Americans will enter psychotherapy at some point in their lives, a figure that puts therapy squarely within the everyday: no longer is a stint in therapy considered a clear sign of mental illness, as it once was. Today, therapy is part of our lives. People go into therapy for help with their love lives, help with their careers, help with their spouses and children. Sometimes people even seek therapy "before the fact." These days an engaged couple may sign on for prenuptial therapy, and I know a father of two, himself a therapist, who is sending both children to therapists in hopes they will grow up to be healthy adults.

The problem is few people realize going in how hard it can be to get back out. Or, as one woman in the throes of leaving therapy put it, "You need therapy to help you get over leaving therapy."

Separation, or "termination"—the professional term that can be daunting, to say the least—is difficult in part because of the unique attachment that grows between therapist and patient. In therapy a "transference" develops, a psychological state in which the patient transfers people and problems from his or her "real life" onto the neutral, professional figure of the therapist. The therapist becomes a stand-in father, mother, lover, teacher—whatever the patient needs his therapist to be in order to work through his problems. Because of transference, leaving therapy is haunted by images of all other leave-takings: when a patient ends therapy he or she is leaving home, or lover, or school all over again. This can hurt.

And beyond transference, there is the simple fact of loss. People grow attached to their therapists for real-world reasons. Perhaps you like your therapist's smile, or his sense of humor, or his diplomatic way of putting things. You esteem him as a real person, not just as a transference figure. Freud called this real attachment the therapeutic alliance and believed that analysis cannot proceed without it. As he saw from the beginning, you have to trust and like your therapist in order to reveal yourself in therapy. Thus, when you face the issue of leaving therapy, you face the issue of loss. If you truly end therapy, you may never see your therapist again. Leaving therapy means saying goodbye.

As for your therapist, termination can be hard for him as well. Because he has his own ties to the patient (called "countertransference"), his feelings about your going may be complicated. Therapists suffer loss, too, and they have to deal with the added possibility that your leaving may signal an implicit criticism of their work. Perhaps you are dissatisfied? Such fugitive thoughts cross the therapist's mind unbidden when it is the patient making the decision to terminate, not he. And given his position as the healthy one, the therapist can hardly ask for reassurance on this score—nor would he want to.

And, of course, there is the highly charged issue of

money. Therapists live under the same financial pres-
sures the rest of us do and, image aside, usually they
are not wealthy people. A therapist in private practice
who has no source of income other than patient fees
must maintain his practice at a certain level in order to
pay his own bills. Unless he is blessed with a lengthy
waiting list, he cannot help but register—if only at an
unconscious level—the fact that your going takes a bite
out of his income. Not that he would try to hold you in
therapy for this reason; it's just that the money factor
makes the subject even more fraught than it already
is—on both sides.

What it all amounts to is a situation in which there
are a potentially overwhelming number of subtle and
not-so-subtle forces working against termination. Feelings are mixed, on both sides. While you do want to
leave—and while your therapist may genuinely want
to help you leave—neither of you can look forward
wholeheartedly to saying farewell. You'd like to stay for
one set of reasons, your therapist would like you to stay
for another, and together you may form an alliance to
prolong therapy.

Or you may find yourself engaged in a struggle over
which one of you—therapist or patient—declares therapy to be at an end. When leaving is entirely the patient's idea, as frequently it is, a therapist may throw
up roadblocks. You are not "ready," he may say, implying that your desire to terminate reveals a wish to run
away from your problems. Or—another common response—your therapist may interpret a desire to leave
therapy as a sign that you cannot "commit" to a relationship.

When you trust and admire your therapist you can
only be deeply affected by such analyses, whether or
not they are true (and "truth" in therapy is always open
to interpretation). You thought you were better and

suddenly you are hearing from your therapist that you are not—worse, that your very desire to leave therapy is a sign that you *need* therapy. Abruptly you see your newfound self-reliance metamorphosing into just another symptom. Faced with a resistant therapist, you must either rebel and declare yourself cured—a process that can be painful indeed—or sink back into business as usual. In the words of one patient, veteran of a prolonged struggle to end her therapy, "Whenever I try to quit therapy I end up going twice a week."

Making matters even more confusing for all concerned is the fact that the psychiatric profession offers no clear-cut guidelines for establishing when therapy is finished. In 1937 Freud wrote that analysts rely on the faculty of intuition to know when therapy is at an end, and little has changed since then. The *Comprehensive Textbook of Psychiatry*, the 3,000-page standard reference work in the field, devotes only 10 pages in total to the subject, and not one of the brief entries on termination suggests that it may be the patient who intuits the end.

This is a book for the patient. If you are trying to leave therapy, or if you are involved with someone who is trying to leave therapy, or if you are simply wondering whether now might be the time—all these dilemmas have been faced by the patients and professionals whose experiences appear in these pages. And if you are thinking of starting therapy yourself, the following chapters will lay out the issues involved in termination *before* you make the commitment to begin.

None of this is meant to discourage you from entering therapy with a good therapist who comes to you well recommended. Starting therapy may turn out to be one of the best decisions you will make: for the vast majority of patients, therapy works—or at the very least it *helps*. The right therapist at the right time in your life can help you change things for the better.

But—and this is crucial—for most patients, therapy works best when it is a finite affair. Interminable therapy in which you spend year after year analyzing the same stories with the same characters and the same endings is the kind of therapy that does not move you forward. Good therapy has a beginning, a middle, and an end, and if you linger in the middle forever, you forfeit the insights and strength a successful termination brings. You *need* to end therapy; you need to finish.

Unfortunately, knowing *when* to finish, and how, is a subject concerning which confusion reigns. No one set of standards or criteria exists that, having been met, means you are ready to leave. Instead, when it comes to termination, you must feel your way.

This book will help. Here you will find the results of two years spent interviewing patients who have left therapy—or who were trying to decide whether the time had come. Some of these patients experienced the ideal termination: a productive leave-taking with both therapist and patient agreeing that the time was right, and with the therapist easing the way. Their stories will show you what a good termination looks like. Other patients did not fare so well. They couldn't make up their minds, they feared what might happen if they left, they just didn't *know*. And a very few patients endured terminations that left them bruised and shaken; these were patients involved with therapists who could not let go.

All of their stories are here. Whatever your situation, you will find that you are not alone—a realization that often helps in and of itself. One of the curious things about termination is that it is the only form of leave-taking nobody really talks about. All other major life partings—divorce, death, growing up and leaving home—are public events. People recognize these passages with cards, ceremonies, legal papers, or tea and sympathy—all of which shore you up as you face your goodbye, *validating* your feelings as real and justified. But leaving therapy is an entirely private experience. No one sends you a card because you have just said goodbye to a therapist you've known for many years; no one even notices. You face what may be a major loss completely alone.

This book will put you in good company. Here you will see that what you are thinking and feeling is much like what every patient thinks and feels about leaving: among patients termination is a universal experience, with universal themes and stages. Also included here is the most current work of research psychologists on the issue of termination, examining when, why, and how patients, in the few formal studies that have been undertaken to date, have left therapy—and what happened to them over the years after that day.

In short, this book will help you sort out the confusion of feelings and concerns every patient meets when approaching termination. And knowing what the end of therapy is all about is crucial to anyone who has ever been in—or who ever *may* be in—therapy. Even if you are only thinking about entering therapy, and are wondering how long it will take and how much change for the better you can expect, you will find answers here. If you have already left therapy but are wondering whether you made the right decision, again, the research collected here should help you know whether you have done as much as you should. And if you are among those thousands of patients presently in therapy who are nearing the moment of saying goodbye, this book will see you through.

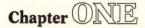

BECOMING A PATIENT

Therapy's catch-22 clicks in at the very beginning: the more successful the start, the harder the end. This is so because the task of therapy's initial stage is to develop what psychologists call the "therapeutic alliance": a strong attachment to your therapist based on affection and trust. You and your therapist join forces and become allies against your problems.

As should be obvious to anyone who has ever been in therapy, this attachment differs considerably from the sort of working alliances we form with other professionals in our lives—with our accountant, say, or our dentist. Obviously, in the case of accountants and dentists our feelings have no effect upon their competence. Suppose your health plan requires you to see a dentist you neither like nor trust; your attitude is not going to make any difference to the ultimate outcome of your root canal. If he's a good dentist, it's a good root canal regardless of the dim view you've taken.

But with a therapist, his competence—his capacity to help—depends directly on your attitude toward him. You can spend fifteen years hashing it out with the

15

finest analyst in the profession, but if you have never come to trust him, you have probably wasted your time.

Trust is widely acknowledged to be essential in the case of insight therapy, which is the dominant form of therapy practiced in America today. (As we will see, however, trust is equally important in all other forms of therapy as well.) As its name implies, insight therapy depends on the patient's getting "in touch" with hidden feelings and perceptions; the patient comes face-to-face with what he is feeling that he does not know he is feeling. And most therapists—most patients, for that matter—agree that insight comes from within. In other words, a patient cannot achieve insight simply by having his therapist tell him outright what's going on within him. He needs to trust and like his therapist in order to arrive at insight *on his own*, with his therapist as witness and guide.

Lee Ann discovered the truth of this proposition during her third course of therapy. At thirty-five, she had already seen two therapists but was still struggling to come to grips with her love life. She wanted a serious relationship with a man but was not finding it. So far, therapy had not helped.

On the face of it, her frustration in love seemed to be merely a matter of missed connections. As she put it, "The men I like aren't attracted to me, and the men who like me—I'm not attracted to them." Several stints in therapy had done little to give her any insight into the reasons behind this pattern, or even to convince her that there *were* reasons involved. To her, the situation felt like simple bad luck.

Finally her third therapist, with whom she had developed a healthy therapeutic alliance, asked her to try a visualization exercise. Lee Ann was to imagine where she would most like to be at that moment, and what she would most like to be doing. To her shock, every image conjured up in her mind's eye was of her alone; no fantasy lovers completed the scene. Apparently, her secret wish was to be alone.

This notion hit her with the force of revelation, despite the fact that for a number of years people close to her had been explicitly suggesting that she did not want a relationship so wholeheartedly as she insisted she did. Until now, she had never bought this explanation for her difficulties. The idea that she suffered from a fear of intimacy—as friends and former therapists saw it—made no sense to her. How could it when her most powerful *conscious* emotion was a longing for love? Invariably she drew a blank when therapists suggested outright that she was in some way *seeking* her solitary state. Her wish for romance was obscuring all other feelings, including her need to be alone. The visualization exercise provided compelling internal evidence that perhaps she did have problems with intimacy. And now this could become, in her mind, a legitimate topic in her therapy. It was a breakthrough.

It was also a breakthrough that happened with a therapist she liked. She had never quite warmed to the other therapists she had seen, and as a result she had been resistant to what they had been trying to get her to see—which was not really much different from what her present therapist was helping her discover. While neither of the others had suggested the visualization exercise, it is likely she would not have come up with such striking results even if they had. Having developed only a weak and rudimentary alliance with them, she—her unconscious, that is—would have blocked the insight. Trusting her new therapist as much as she did allowed her to open up.

The point is, Lee Ann's experience holds true for anyone who is seeing a therapist: a good therapeutic alliance is crucial to making contact with your own buried thoughts, dreams, and fears.

All forms of insight therapy (which is what Lee Ann's therapist practiced) are based on some notion of the unconscious. Perhaps unconsciously you fear intimacy; unconsciously you fear success; unconsciously you are drawn to men who resemble your father or to women who resemble your mother; and so on.

The unconscious is important even in cognitive therapy, though some cognitive therapists would argue the point. Unlike the various forms of insight therapy, cognitive therapy assumes that a patient's thoughts—his *conscious* thoughts—about life depress him more than life does itself. Because cognitive therapy has become a major force, especially in the treatment of depression, it deserves special mention here. How different, truly, is cognitive therapy from any other form of Freudian-inspired therapy?

In actual practice, it is not that different. The theory behind it differs radically from the theory of psychoanalysis, but the form cognitive theory takes inside the therapeutic session is quite similar. A cognitive therapist, who simply wants to change his client's way of *thinking* about the world, still has to go through the work of helping his client sort out what, in fact, he *does* think about the world. Implicitly, cognitive therapists recognize an unconscious just as surely as do Freudians; cognitive therapists, like psychoanalysts, accept the premise that large areas of our hearts and minds are dark to us.

The difference lies in the why. Psychoanalysts believe in repression, a psychic force whose purpose is to keep unconscious thoughts and feelings unconscious. In contrast, cognitive therapists believe in what they term "automatic thoughts"—thoughts that occur so quickly and so sketchily that though they are technically conscious, we do not really notice them.

Where the psychoanalytically oriented therapist will encourage some form of free association in hopes of tapping into repressed thoughts, the cognitive psychologist will ask his patient to examine exactly what he is thinking about life that is making him so troubled. As an example, Dr. Aaron T. Beck, one of the major proponents of cognitive therapy, offers the case of a patient who sees an old friend and at once feels unaccountably sad. Using the cognitive approach his therapist asks him to recall precisely what thoughts immediately preceded his sad feeling. He does, and his thoughts turn out to be quite saddening: "If I greet Bob, he may not remember me....He may snub me....It's been so long, we won't have anything in common. It won't be like old times." These thoughts are only half-conscious, but they *are* conscious nonetheless. The patient can retrieve them. The cognitive therapist, like the more traditional psychodynamic therapist, is searching for hidden mental contents—the difference is simply a matter of degree.

Thus, when it comes to the actual practice of therapy, Freudian patient and cognitive "client" (the term cognitive therapists tend to prefer) turn out to be treated in much the same way. Simple, direct analyses offered by a therapist are not going to budge either the repressed Freudian unconscious or the deeply ingrained cognitive belief system. The phrase "fear of intimacy" coming from a total stranger—your new therapist— simply does not make sense no matter what that stranger's philosophical orientation. Your defense mechanisms—or simply your capacity for conviction, depending on your therapist's theoretical leanings—

block it. In either form of therapy you need to develop a strong therapeutic alliance for it to work. You need to trust and like your therapist, whatever his approach.

What is most impressive about the therapeutic alliance is that it keeps patients coming back even when they would rather not. As Lee Ann discovered, knowledge is painful: what woman really wants to know—as Lee Ann finally had to know—that she has always, all her life, felt abandoned by father and mother both? Felt unloved and unloving? These are not cheering revelations. Much better simply to hold on to the plausible belief that "all the good ones are married," which is what Lee Ann had been telling herself for years.

If a patient's therapeutic alliance does not develop sufficiently, this is precisely what he will do: hold tight to the rationalizations that explain—and preserve— the status quo. A successful therapeutic alliance keeps you coming back—in every sense—to confront painful truths when you would otherwise withdraw, ensuring your continued physical attendance at therapy as well as your emotional attendance. A good therapeutic alliance keeps you emotionally engaged, emotionally present, even when engagement becomes hurtful.

Obviously, no other professional relationship shows such tenacity; when things get rocky with your dentist, no one expects you to keep coming back hoping for better days. But when sessions with your therapist grow painful, not only are you expected to tough it out, you are encouraged to see your pain as an actual *good*—as a sign that progress is being made. As we will see, however, an alliance so powerful that it can survive months of difficult sessions is a hard one to break. Like marriage, and like parenthood, therapy is a for-better-for-worse proposition.

In order to see exactly *how* difficult it is to part with a therapist—and how to go about doing it—we have to know exactly what the therapeutic relationship consists of. What makes it so uniquely powerful?

Trust. To begin with, a good therapeutic alliance involves enormous trust. Most therapists agree that the therapeutic alliance is strongest when the patient believes the therapist to be always and forever *on his side,* and interested at all times in what he has to say about himself.

In contrast, marriage does not offer such absolutes. It cannot, because at the very least married people have moods. Husbands and wives are more supportive some days than others. But the therapist can be counted on to be equally there for his patients in each and every session. Unlike the spouse, the therapist does not throw curves, ever—or is not supposed to. You know that if you come to therapy depressed or anxious day after day for weeks on end, your therapist will always have the same response: empathy, calm, concern. But when you come *home* depressed day after day it is a different matter. Realistically, no spouse can compete with a therapist on empathy, if only because marriage is a full-time relationship, while the therapeutic relationship is confined to just one or two hours a week.

More compelling yet, in therapy the patient is always center stage. In this respect, the therapeutic alliance is more like a parent-child relationship, the closest you can come to a bond that is (or is supposed to be) absolute, in which one person is always there for you, no matter what his or her own needs and feelings may be. The therapeutic relationship approximates the unconditional love—or at least the unconditional there-ness —we associate with parenthood. Not surprisingly, patients may come to trust their therapists in much the same unquestioning way that children trust their parents. This makes the therapeutic alliance powerful indeed.

Consistency. Unconditional there-ness involves a subtler pleasure as well: the pleasure of consistency. Trust is based on predictability; when you trust someone, you trust that person always—or generally—to react as you expect him to. Therapists, because of the limited time and controlled circumstances in which they see patients, are quite possibly the most predictable people on earth. Their years of training have honed to perfection a professional consistency of manner and approach. Therapy textbooks include transcripts of sessions that are scrutinized for the most subtle departure from the appropriate course, the message to the novice therapist being that any such departures make for bad therapy. Therapists are not allowed to get up on the wrong side of the bed. They are not allowed to be different from one day to the next.

At the emotional level, the therapist's utter sameness feeds back into his trustworthiness. Sheer consistency makes a therapist trustworthy—more so than the mere changeable mortals we number among our friends and family, people we see in many and various moods and attitudes.

Intimacy. Starting therapy may also call up another powerful relational experience: falling in love. As therapy begins, intimacy develops with incredible speed. Suddenly, within moments of meeting your therapist, you are revealing aspects of yourself that even your nearest and dearest may not know about. The only other time a relationship gets such a running start is when on a first date the talk catches fire at once between lovers-to-be. The definition of Mr. or Ms. Right is often a person to whom you can talk immediately as if the two of you had known each other all your lives. This is precisely what patients do in first sessions with therapists, which only adds to the tenacity of the therapeutic bond. From the outset, on this score as on so many others, therapy shows a kinship with the most powerful relationships we know.

As well it should—therapists are *trained* to make themselves into highly appealing people. In any text on the practice of therapy you will find therapists at pains to start off the therapeutic relationship on the right foot. They are taught to listen empathetically, never to appear arrogant or judgmental in any way, to avoid placing themselves in a superior position vis-à-vis the patient—in short, to do everything in their power to inspire trust and liking. The therapist woos the patient, and the patient responds. The bond is formed, and it is a very tough one to break.

Thus inside therapy trust, consistency, and immediate intimacy make for a strong attachment. But one outside factor contributes as well: therapy's public image.

Put simply, therapy has had good press. People enter therapy fully expecting to find a therapist who will be receptive and consistent in every session. And as countless studies have shown, expectations profoundly affect perception. Enter therapy expecting your therapist to be trustworthy and consistent, and you will interpret his or her behavior in terms of those expectations. He will not have as far to go to win your trust as others you may encounter in everyday life.

The striking thing about therapy's popular image is that the same psychologists and other experts who see the marital relationship as inherently imperfect routinely encourage us to expect the therapeutic relationship to be, if not perfect, then certainly a lot more per· fect than marriage or family or any other significant relationship outside therapy. Invariably, therapy is offered as the solution to the problems marriage and family inevitably produce.

To be fair, of course, experts do not tell us that therapy will be perfect in terms of its effectiveness. Therapy, it is said, can change us only if we want to change, and only if we work hard to change. In the popular conception of therapy, change is the patient's responsibility. In short, the ultimate *results* of therapy are not idealized by the media.

However, the *process* of therapy is. In the popular imagination the therapeutic relationship, unlike any other, is taken to be reliable. The same media sources admonishing readers that "nobody's perfect" imply that some therapists *are*, that you can get from a therapist what you can never get from a mate: total consistency, total concern, perfect there-ness.

Very likely, this public belief stems from the therapist's standing as a professional. The therapist *has* to be there for you—it's his job. The confidence good parents and good spouses formerly inspired has been shifted to therapists in the professionalization of once private family functions noted by social historian Christopher Lasch.

Even further, when it comes to relationships, therapy is promoted as the court of final appeal. It is the meta-relationship, which stands apart from and above all normal, troubled human relationships. It is always the solution, (almost) never the problem.

At least, this is what people come into therapy *expecting*. Therapists recognize this expectation, and have produced volumes on the subject of the patient's idealization of the therapist—which they attribute to the psychological phenomenon of transference. But in fact this idealization is structured into the cultural view of therapy. Magazines and books and television talk shows tout the virtues of therapy long before any individual patient turns up for help.

None of this is lost on the patient. As Bernie Zilbergeld found when he interviewed former therapy patients for his book *The Shrinking of America*, most of them leave therapy feeling very positive about their experience—even when all of their original problems remain. People believe in therapy, and believing in therapy can make leaving it hard.

Ending therapy would be difficult enough even if all you had to contend with was your strong attachment to a valued and trusted therapist who has done you good. But, in fact, when it comes to leaving therapy you encounter another major obstacle as well: your status vis-à-vis your therapist. Broadly speaking, patients tend to feel somewhat below their therapists—whether this takes the form of the layperson looking up to the expert, the patient looking up to the doctor, or even the child looking up to the wise adult. And it can be very hard to make a major life decision from a position of "inferiority."

Therapists are well aware of this phenomenon, which, once again, they attribute to transference. The patient, therapists believe, transfers mother and father onto the therapist—then looks up to him, rebels against him, generally plunges into whatever scenario with him that he needs to work out in relation to his real parents. As researcher and psychotherapist Hans Strupp puts it in his excellent text on short-term therapy, *Psychotherapy in a New Key*, "the patient tends to cast himself or herself in the role of the helpless child vis-à-vis a powerful parent in the (futile) hope that in so doing the original problem will have a different outcome." Notice the language: the patient *casts himself*, rather than *is cast* by therapy. This is transference.

However, the truth is that therapy itself pushes the patient into a childlike role just as surely as the patient unconsciously adopts this role. Put simply, when you enter therapy you undergo a subtle—but very real—drop in status, a drop from "normal person" to patient. And in the process of assuming the patient identity, you inevitably cede some authority over yourself, *by definition*. You are, in some sense, handing yourself over to an expert.

Of course, most patients—and most therapists—bristle at the mention of status. Patients prefer to think of themselves as being on equal footing with their therapists, and certainly most members of the profession are at pains to discourage any felt difference in status. According to Strupp:

> The therapist's stance should be that of a reasonable, mature, and trustworthy fellow adult who fosters a *symmetrical* relationship between equals. The patient should never have the experience of being treated as an object, a case, the bearer of a disorder or disease....

• However, real limits exist as to how much symmetry can be created in a context in which one person needs help and the other person gives it. The therapist *expects* the patient to idealize him and then, paradoxically, is instructed to treat this worshipful creature as an equal. In other words, the therapist is enjoined to treat as an equal a patient who will not see him as one. At heart, this is a species of noblesse oblige. Treating an insecure, anxious being as an equal is a quite different proposition from treating a self-confident, self-sufficient being as an equal.

Inevitably, this difference comes across to the patient. For one thing, having a therapist show nonstop care and concern for you, soothing as this may be, does have the paradoxical effect of confirming the fact that you are in need of care and concern. Never mind the reality that you have sought therapy precisely because you *are* troubled; confirmation of your distress is still unsettling.

It is unsettling, in part, because being troubled does not put you in a position of strength. It is hard to feel equal to anyone, let alone your therapist, when you are at utter low ebb—which is where many people are when they go into therapy, especially first-timers, who are often so resistant to the idea of treatment that they put it off until things are really dire. Of his decision to enter therapy one man told me he had been so depressed for so long that he found himself passing his days sitting on his apartment floor, weeping. Another man had become overwhelmingly anxious, to the point where the most fleeting contact with waiters in restaurants provoked him to uncontrollable outbursts—he was dressing down waiters all over town.

It is easy to see that neither of these men is going to feel the ready equal of a calm and rational therapist who gives every appearance of being in control of himself and his life. And while people who are returning to therapy for a second or third time may do so in a much more reasonable, self-aware fashion, they, too, are probably not in the best of psychic shape at the moment of actually entering therapy.

In short, even the most sensitive of therapists cannot make a new patient feel equal simply by treating him as an equal. What is more likely is that the depressed or anxious patient will begin to feel grateful for the therapist's respectful behavior toward him, rather than merely take it as his due. Such a patient ends up feeling not so much like an "object" or a "case" as like *an object or a case that is being treated as a person.*

And the truth is, a new patient *is* a case. The first meeting between therapist and patient is diagnostic; the therapist, in listening to the new patient, is trying to get a fix on his or her problems. To do so, the well-trained therapist listens analytically. He or she does not take at face value what the patient says, but instead searches for hidden meanings and concerns. A female patient who asks a number of questions about precisely what kind of therapy her doctor offers, for example, may be seen as expressing an unspoken fear that the therapist will try to dominate her—this in session number one. While a good therapist will be *right* in making this interpretation, the very fact of being so right so fast can be daunting to his patient. To have a total stranger know something about you in five minutes that you had not realized after twenty, thirty, or forty years can be unnerving.

Moreover, in therapy, interpretation is not a two-way street. Much of what the patient says is assumed to mean something else, while everything the therapist says is assumed to mean exactly what he says it means. This is not equality. True equals do not second-guess each other, and if they do, both parties get to second-guess each other equally.

Intensifying the psychological effect of knowing yourself to be the needy, symptomatic one is the simple physical reality of taking yourself off to a "doctor's" office once or twice a week. If you did not feel "sick" when you made your first appointment, you are likely to begin to feel sick now that you see yourself sitting in a medical waiting room. Diane, a then-unemployed book editor who entered therapy in her late twenties, recalls her own discomfiture at finding herself keeping new, neurotic company.

Because Diane could not afford a therapist in private

practice she was being seen at a vastly reduced fee by a resident at a local teaching hospital, where none of the usual doctor's office amenities were available. Normally, therapists in private practice select offices with separate entrances and exits so that patients need not pass each other on the way in or out. The reasons for such an office design became clear to Diane when confronted with her resident's crowded—and dramatic— waiting room. Patients of all stripes were gathered there, many of them clearly on medication, many of them clearly not responding to medication. Mothers trying desperately to placate impossibly overweight and raging teenage daughters; lone, grubby men muttering to themselves in far corners—it was a disheartening scene to say the least. And Diane was *part of it*. Worse yet, at one point her psychiatrist was temporarily assigned to a veterans' hospital, which meant Diane had to find a seat on the torn and patched vinyl sofas where hospitalized vets sat hour after hour watching reruns of *Kojak*. Not only did she get to contemplate the shambles she felt her own life to be (no job, no man), she had to sit there thinking about what Vietnam had done to the American soldier as well. Invariably she felt worse just moments after taking her place in the waiting room than she had the entire week before.

But the most painful aspect of the arrangement may have been Diane's weekly encounters with her doctor's preceding patient. "I knew who she was," says Diane, "because every week she would come back into the waiting room after her session to make her next appointment with Dr. ———. I used to always look her over out of the corner of my eye." What Diane saw depressed her. The patient was a young woman in her twenties who invariably wore the same thing, an Empire-waisted minidress the likes of which had not been seen since the '60s. Her appearance was so out of keeping with anything young women her age were currently wearing (this was before miniskirts had made their comeback) that she looked radically disconnected from any conceivable social group. She looked eccentric, to put it as generously as possible.

And when she spoke she quickly surpassed mere eccentricity. To Diane she seemed to be at least borderline delusional, judging by the non sequiturs dotting her exchanges with the clerks. "Basically," says Diane, "she just came across as truly crazy. Not upset, not neurotic. Crazy. I felt bad for her, but every time she came in from her appointment my heart would just sink. I would think, This is the kind of patient my doctor sees. These are my people; this is *my group*."

Clearly, for Diane, simply going to her appointments —physically showing up and waiting for them— amounted to a precipitous drop in *felt* status. And this drop in status led directly to a decline in self-esteem, in spite of the fact that her therapist's demeanor was invariably warm, supportive, and respectful. Inside her therapy session Diane felt better about herself, but immediately outside she felt much worse. Later on she would come to wonder whether the wear on her self-image was making it hard for her to believe she could make it on her own, without her therapist. Sitting each week in the bedlam that was his waiting room, she could not help but wonder whether any of the patients he saw were ever going to function outside therapy. And if nobody else was going to make it—and from what she could see nobody seemed likely to—what grounds did she have to think that she was going to be the *one?*

All in all, when you go into therapy you don't just receive therapy. Unavoidably you also take on a new cultural role: you *become a patient*. Even when your therapist's office—and your therapist's manner—is carefully designed to minimize your new standing as patient, you can't help but feel the shift. A sense that you are a patient, and that patients (often) are sick people, may shadow your time in therapy.

Diane's experience reveals the danger in coming to think of yourself as a patient. As much as what goes on inside therapy can shore up your self-esteem, the mere fact of *being a patient* tends to undermine it. And since self-esteem is basic to all decision-making, the decision about when to leave therapy can become that much more difficult, more difficult than the decision to enter in the first place. Becoming a patient can make becoming an ex-patient hard.

WORKING THROUGH

Deciding whether and when to leave therapy is difficult because of the very real possibility that you could be making a mistake: you could be leaving too soon. Moreover, the entire issue grows especially murky when the reason you want to leave is that you are dissatisfied with your progress. The problem is, dissatisfaction in and of itself is not sufficient grounds to leave because, paradoxically, good therapy can *feel* bad. "Dissatisfaction" can arise either because your therapy is genuinely not very helpful, *or* because your therapy *is* helpful and you are resisting. So, to make a sound decision about staying or going, you need to know what good therapy looks like—even when it may feel like an unhappy experience.

As we have seen, the therapeutic relationship revolves around *transference*. Semiconsciously, the patient transfers feelings and expectations from past relationships onto the present relationship with the therapist, who becomes a stand-in father, mother, lover, friend.

Therapy takes off from here. Because you reenact

your characteristic—and problematic—relationship patterns with your therapist, he or she can see exactly what those problematic patterns are. You can then "work them through" inside the privacy of the therapeutic session.

As a simplified example, say you grew up with harsh, rejecting parents. As an adult you continue to expect harsh, rejecting treatment from those you love. Worse, you *position* those you love as harsh rejectors; that is, you act as if you expect them to reject you. Maybe you grow defensive before the other person has actually done anything to make you defensive, maybe you cringe whenever a loved one opens a conversation with "I'd like to talk to you about something," maybe you reject new friends and lovers before they get a chance to reject you. Whatever form it takes, you are setting up the people you love as rejectors, and once in therapy you transfer this constellation of behaviors, attitudes, longings, and fears onto your therapist. He, too, becomes—in your eyes—a harsh, rejecting figure. This then provides the material of your therapy, the material you are working on.

It is probably safe to say that all therapists believe in some version of transference, whether or not they emphasize it in practice. Freud believed that transference was at the heart of psychoanalysis. In Freud's day the analyst encouraged his patient's transference by maintaining a strict neutrality in manner, appearance, and language—hence the famous inexpressiveness of the classical psychoanalyst, and the practice of answering a question with a question. (Patient: "Where are you going on vacation?" Analyst: "You seem interested in my vacation. Has something reminded you of vacation time?") The point of being neutral was to strip the analyst of personality, thus forcing the patient to transfer other people's personalities onto him in order to make any sense of him at all. In other words, since the analyst had no discernible character of his own, he became a blank "screen" onto which the patient could project the images of important people in his life outside therapy. The neutral analyst then became the decidedly nonneutral father/mother/sister/brother/lover/spouse. Once installed in any one of these positions, the analyst could then witness, and analyze, his patient's problems.

In some sense transference is the dark side of the therapeutic alliance. Where the alliance is ideally the rational, adult connection with the therapist, the transference is the less rational, more childlike attachment. Thus the patient relates to his therapist on two fronts: he sees both the "good" therapist (with whom he is allied) and the "bad" therapist (who represents all the difficult people in his private life). By its very nature, therapy involves ambivalence; it is a love-hate affair.

Resistance is a third component of therapy. Therapists believe that all patients, inevitably, will resist therapy. Patients choose therapy, but then they fight it. They fight it because they have got the therapist tangled up with conflict-ridden figures from the rest of their lives —and they are now fighting the same old family/love-life battles anew with their therapist.

They also fight therapy because truth hurts. Most therapists believe that patients are people who suffer from unconscious conflicts, which they cover up with conscious rationales and "maladaptive" behavior patterns. In therapy, these conscious rationales and maladaptive behaviors form the basis of resistance. Somewhat paradoxically, the patient does not want to let go of his standard—if painful—way of doing and seeing things.

Maureen, like Lee Ann, went into therapy to try to

work out her love life. She, too, harbored many fears about what real closeness with a man would bring, while at the same time longing for an intimate relationship. In time, and with the help of an expert therapist, Maureen came to see that she was, in fact, suffering from a buried conflict concerning her parents. Put simply, she was in competition with her mother for her father's love. Competition with one's mother being a no-win proposition, Maureen unconsciously feared that if she won her father she would lose her mother. The result for her grown-up love life was devastating: essentially, Maureen was making sure she never *got* the man in order to protect her psychic position as her mother's daughter.

However, coming to this recognition was not easy, and Maureen resisted her therapist straight down the line, primarily by playing out her destructive romantic patterns inside therapy, too. Maureen was a woman who characteristically fell for withdrawn men. For their part, these men were initially attracted by her adoration of them, but then disappeared when she began to make emotional demands of her own. Because a therapist is by definition "withdrawn"—a therapist is absolutely forbidden by the canons of his profession to fall in love with patients—Maureen readily transferred this expectation onto her own doctor. She went into therapy lavishly admiring her therapist—just as she lavishly admired all her lovers at first. Then, around two months later, she began to be furious with him for remaining emotionally distant (again, just at the point where, in a love affair, she would begin to feel rage toward the latest withdrawn man she had chosen).

"One of my worst moments in therapy," recalls Maureen, "was the day I finally worked up enough nerve to tell my therapist about a sexual fantasy I had had about him. He reacted without any feeling whatsoever—just his usual therapy reserve—and suddenly I saw red. I felt like, Why am I paying eighty dollars an hour to get rejected when I can get rejected in real life for free?"

Needless to say, Maureen's was a classic transference reaction—called the "transference neurosis" by professionals. Her therapist had become a stand-in for the unresponsive men in her life, and Maureen reacted to him accordingly. She became so angry that she refused to open up any further for a time. In short, Maureen resisted therapy *by means of her transference,* as do all patients. Furthermore, she resisted not just because in "real life" she resisted all men in the same way, but also because she did not want to examine what her behavior might mean. A part of her did not *want* to start having peaceable relations with men, because that would mean the loss of her mother. Remember that the resistance *protects* precious, if destructive, solutions to major life problems. When her destructive pattern with men was threatened by therapy, Maureen resisted.

The bulk of therapy is devoted to a task called "working through the resistance," which means coming to terms with destructive patterns of behavior. The patient slowly comes to recognize what she is doing, perhaps to understand why she feels compelled to do it, and ultimately to stop doing it, to change. That is what eventually happened to Maureen, who, when she left therapy two years later, had finally fallen in love with an emotionally present man. In the process she had stopped feeling so angry at and hurt by her therapist. The old pattern had been broken.

But before reaching this point, as we have seen, Maureen inevitably became angry. Anger is a cornerstone of therapy. Therapists believe that somewhere in the middle of therapy all patients get angry with their therapists. If a patient does not become angry, if all is hearts and flowers, then treatment probably is not progressing.

This belief stems from the therapeutic assumption that all emotional difficulties can be traced back to faulty relationships among people. Whether you have trouble relating to the opposite sex, completing assigned projects, or getting up in the morning, these problems are all assumed to be, at some level, "people" problems. Say your trouble is work-related: you procrastinate, miss deadlines. This might seem to be a problem strictly between you and yourself, but a therapist will look for the interpersonal origins of your procrastination. Perhaps your parents were overly demanding when you were a child, leading you to put off judgment day by never completing anything that would have to stand judgment. This is the sort of "people" explanation therapy will bring to light. It will also look to see how your present relationships support your "bad habits." Perhaps your procrastination frustrates and infuriates an overbearing colleague, who has become the stand-in for your parents—transference in the workplace!

In any event, working through this problem will inevitably involve anger, which therapists tend to see as a healing emotion. Their reasoning goes like this: Most patients have been let down by important past relationships—whether with parents, lovers, or friends. Even if they had model parents, children feel let down simply by the fact that they cannot be center stage every moment of their childhood. Hence the phrase "infantile rage." Children, it is thought, become angry when forced to share their parents' attention with others, or when parents frustrate their wishes by disciplining them.

Although parents understand that anger is a natural

reaction on their children's part, the children come to see that they must control their anger—tantrums are not okay. Parents respond variously to children's anger by growing angry themselves, by sending the child to his room, by taking away the child's toys if he breaks them in a fit, and so on. The child inevitably gets the message (however unintended) that anger threatens his happy relationship with his parents, if only for those moments he spends cooling off in his room. Anger *disrupts.*

In adult life many of us, having learned that anger is a dangerous emotion, deal with the feeling only indirectly. Perhaps we hide our anger altogether, perhaps we engage in "passive aggression," perhaps we redirect anger to safe targets (the "kick the dog" phenomenon). As a result we may not know when we are angry—or, when we do know, we may not recognize exactly what we are angry *about.*

This is where the therapist comes in. He believes that whatever your problem, it has something to do with unfulfilled needs about which you harbor long-standing anger. The therapist gets at those needs by getting at your anger. As you move into the middle of therapy, you begin to transfer and to express the anger you have felt at other major figures in your life.

The *focus* of your anger helps you and your therapist understand the nature of your problems. Talk to five different patients all seeing the same therapist and you will probably hear five different reasons for being angry with him. For Lee Ann it was her therapist's lack of emotion, for another patient his supposed judgmentalism; for another it might have been his seeming unsupportiveness. Each patient grows angry with his therapist for a reason having specifically to do with his own life patterns.

A good therapist refuses to take the bait. Often, patients are accustomed to people responding in very particular ways to their anger. Locked into a destructive pattern, they are essentially choosing to associate with people who will *continue* to react in that particular way. The therapist attempts to break the pattern. If a patient is used to people walking out, the therapist does not walk out. If the patient is accustomed to people getting furious right back at him, the therapist does not get furious. But most important, the therapist does not leave. He holds steady throughout the middle course of therapy in order to show his patient that relationships are sturdier than he might think. The patient can get mad and his therapist won't disappear.

The hope is that, as the patient feels more certain of his therapist, he will begin to loosen his grip on his customary patterns. Maureen, for example, was utterly convinced that men disappear when you make demands. This was reality to her, and at first therapy seemed to confirm it. But as her therapy went on, and her therapist did not end their relationship even though she was making many demands, she began to see things differently. True, her therapist was not granting her the intimacy she desired. He would not reveal himself to her, hold her, love her. He was unavailable; he was not meeting her demands. But he was not flying the coop because of her demands, and that was crucial to Maureen's learning to trust—and ultimately to choosing a different sort of man.

If Maureen's therapist actually had met her demands, he would have ended up confirming her beliefs about men. Say he had agreed to suspend all the customary rules surrounding the therapeutic relationship and, breaking with propriety, had become her best friend, lover—whatever she desired. And into the bargain, say he promised *not* to be like all the others. While this approach might have been immensely pleasurable for a time, it would have been bad therapy. Maureen's capacity to re-create her pattern would have prevailed. Either her demands would have escalated to the point where her therapist/lover would have been forced to back away, or she would have lost interest in him when she saw that he had made himself a slave to her need. With either outcome her *modus operandi* would have remained the same, and since unconsciously she *wanted* to cling to her familiar pattern, her therapist would, in fact, have played directly into her hands. He would have allowed her to use therapy to *stay* troubled.

Only within the confines of formal therapy could Maureen's view of men and herself begin to alter. Her therapist remained stubbornly professional; he did not return intimacies, nor did he withdraw. Maureen did not get everything she needed, but she was getting some of what she needed—and, more important, the situation was stable. She could get furious, cry, clam up—whatever—and her therapist did not disappear. Thus she began to see that a man (or any important person) could be there. Not necessarily there in every way she wanted him to be, but reliably and sturdily there. She began to see men in a new light, or to notice men she hadn't perceived before. Her expectations began to rise—and lower—simultaneously.

She also began to behave differently toward the men she met out in the real world. Since she was beginning to see that a man won't do everything for you no matter how much you adore him, she began to be a bit less adoring from the start. She became more realistic and confident in her dealings with men, since she was also beginning to see that even if a man couldn't do everything she wanted, he *could* do the main thing, which was to stay with her and care. She gave different signals to the men she dated, and finally began to attract a different sort of man as well.

All of this happened without Maureen's being entirely aware of it, which is where the real art of therapy comes in. The good therapist engages in exceedingly delicate prodding. Therapy is all about tact and timing; no therapist ever simply comes out with a blunt analysis. Instead, he constantly gauges the patient's readiness to consider an interpretation and, when the patient seems receptive, expresses his interpretations in the mildest of terms. Jargon is frowned upon: the patient must not be made to feel like a case.

Thus, when Maureen first reacted with hurt and anger at her therapist's unshakable calm, he did not push it. Instead of interpreting her feelings he confirmed them, saying that he could see she felt angry and that it *is* a difficult situation when someone does not return your desire. In short, he validated her emotion. Only later, when she was more open to examining her response, did he ask her to make the connection between her reaction to him and her customary reaction to the men she dated.

Maureen's therapy provides a perfect example of "working through" a problem. Tactfully and delicately the good therapist helps the patient come to his own understanding by continually directing him to examine the parallels between therapy and life. And, as the patient begins to do things differently in life, he gradually loosens his grip on the therapist, coming to see him more as a therapist, pure and simple. When Maureen started dating a more emotionally present man, she began to understand what her therapist was trying to get across. She came to appreciate his professional reserve; she saw how essential it was to breaking the usual pattern of her relationships.

All told, the middle of therapy is usually a period of intense attachment to the therapist. It can't be otherwise: you are tied to him by bonds of strong affection, as well as bonds of strong resentment—an emotional double whammy. You move into the final stage of therapy when you start to *disengage*—or, more accurately, to be able to disengage. To let go.

If therapy could work precisely according to theory, leaving would not be as hard as it is; certainly it would not be as complicated. The patient would simply sign on, develop the transference neurosis (alongside the therapeutic alliance), work through the transference neurosis, then sign out, burdened only by the sadness of saying goodbye to a therapist he very much liked. The patient would resolve the transference while leaving the alliance intact. But in actual practice, working through the transference is not so clear-cut a process, chiefly because it can be difficult in therapy to distinguish what is *transference* from what is *real*.

Suppose, for example, you see your therapist as a harsh and punitive father. This is not entirely a function of your own personal "pathology." There are also a number of very real situational factors—his age, dress, manner of speech—*asking* you to see him as *some* kind of father (the harsh and punitive part may well come from you and you alone). This puts you into a real bind when it comes to working through your transference: how do you resolve reality? If real factors are pushing you to experience your therapist as a father, how do you move beyond that?

More confusing yet, you may not get much help from your therapist on this kind of resolution. Therapists tend to chalk up their patients' feelings about and perceptions of therapy to transference pure and simple, not to anything they themselves are doing to make their patients feel as they do.

This attitude is, however, inconsistent given the psychotherapeutic notion of *countertransference*—the feelings the *doctor* brings to therapy. These days most professionals believe that no therapist can make himself truly neutral, as Freud urged, because no doctor arrives at therapy devoid of his own feelings, attitudes, and expectations. But therapy texts do not define countertransference as simply the counterpart of transference, or the therapist projecting his or her *own* past relationships onto the present interaction with the patient. Professionals do recognize such a phenomenon, but they also speak of countertransference in a second, quite different sense, referring to the feelings, reactions, and perceptions the patient *evokes* in his therapist.

Therapists pay attention to these "countertransference reactions" because, so the argument goes, if the patient consistently irritates (or flatters or upsets) the therapist, it is a safe bet the patient is irritating or flattering or upsetting everyone else in his life in the same way. The therapist is urged to consider his own feelings about the patient—his countertransference—as useful information concerning the patient's life outside therapy.

A good example of this is Bill's experience after some years of therapy. He was an assistant professor caught up in the midst of a tenure battle. He had recently published his first book, which was the main requirement for earning tenure, and naturally the subject of his book came up frequently in his sessions. One day he mentioned the name of his publisher in passing, as he had done on numerous occasions in the past, and his therapist interrupted to ask who he had said his pub-

lisher was. His publisher was Harcourt, Brace, Jovano-
vich, Bill said. Why? His psychiatrist replied that he
was surprised. He thought Bill had been published by a
"small Southern press."

A small Southern press is a considerable demotion
from Harcourt, and Bill pointed this out in his next
session. Why was his own therapist perceiving his work
as less than it was? This was exactly the problem Bill
was having with a certain senior member of his depart-
ment—a man who was trying to block Bill's tenure—
and he wasn't about to accept the same attitude in his
doctor, who was, after all, supposed to be on his side.
Bill's psychiatrist responded with an appeal to countertransference: the reason he had thought Bill's book
had been published by an obscure press was that Bill
presented himself and his work in this overly modest,
self-denigrating way. In other words, Bill himself had
called forth this reaction in his psychiatrist. He and
Bill then devoted the rest of the session to analyzing
why Bill would make himself appear to be less than he
was.

This line of reasoning does make a great deal of sense,
but notice that in such a scenario countertransference
becomes something someone else can do *to* you: the patient *makes* the therapist feel certain feelings. Bill
made—or encouraged—his therapist to think less of
him. From the patient's point of view, if he can wield
this sort of power over his therapist, surely his therapist—not to mention the entire professional setting of
therapy—must enjoy the same power over him. In
short, if countertransference can happen *to* the therapist, then logically transference can happen *to* his patient.

And in fact it does, from the very beginning. The
hallmarks of therapy—receptiveness, consistency, and

so on—all exert a "transferential pull" on the new patient and call up his experience of parents, family, lovers, friends. For example, some therapists explicitly see themselves as "remothering" their patients, in the belief that patients' real mothers have left something out. If the therapist herself is having this thought, it can hardly be pure transference in the classic sense when the patient has the same thought. The patient has very perceptively picked up on the therapist's unspoken philosophy.

All told, a fair amount of what passes for transference is, in fact, *perception*. And this is why therapy can become terribly confusing; is what you think of your therapist (and therapy) true, or is it transferred? When it comes time to leave, this is a major issue because by rights you should not leave therapy until your transference has been resolved. But if your supposed transference is actually based (at least in part) on a perception of reality, it cannot be resolved. You cannot resolve away reality.

Consider Fran's experience. She began therapy when she was at a total loss about how to live her life. Nearing thirty, she had just left a second career field without having gotten off the ground in either; her one long-term relationship with a man had ended a year before. Concerned, her parents offered to pay for therapy. Fran agreed. Her sister recommended a therapist and she went for her first appointment. When she arrived she discovered that the doctor, a woman, lived in a large and solid upper-middle-class home, complete with well-tended flower beds, a housekeeper, and a BMW parked in front. The woman's offices, located in a guest house, were tastefully appointed, and there was clear evidence of a husband on the premises.

All this was hard on Fran, who at that point felt like a complete loser. Worse, to have this therapist chosen

for her by her older sister—a highly successful busi-
nesswoman who had married into a family of inherited
wealth—appeared to be confirmation by her sister of
her own complete lack of success in any realm. Nevertheless, she signed on with this therapist and ultimately became overwhelmingly attached—so much so,
in fact, that she came to innately have more confidence
in what the doctor had to say than in what she herself
had to say.

From a therapist's perspective, Fran's overawed attitude was a symptom of her transference neurosis, but
from an outsider's perspective there was a bit more
going on. While the transference elements of Fran's relationship with her therapist are obvious—the therapist was associated with a highly successful and
privileged elder sibling—it is also clear that much of
what Fran felt was solidly based in reality. The contrast
between the therapist's existence and Fran's was real
and blatant; it could only underline Fran's feelings of
inferiority. It is not a neurosis to perceive that someone
else is better off than you are, and if it is not a neurosis,
it cannot be "worked through." You cannot resolve
away vast differences in wealth, nor can you resolve
away the fact that your therapist has a home, husband,
and family, while you don't. Fran's therapist, and her
therapy, were *evoking* a feeling of inferiority in Fran.
Even the hardiest of women would feel much the same
if she had to confront this vision of personal and professional success weekly when she herself was alone and
between jobs.

The point is, some of your seeming transference reactions to therapy and your therapist are very real, which
means you could spend the next ten years trying to resolve them with no success. Yes, you need to resolve
your neurotic transference as part of leaving therapy—
but the fact is, you are probably *never* going to know

which parts of your attachment to therapy and to your therapist are coming from transference, which are coming from reality, and which are irresistible—and irreducible—mixtures of both. When it comes to the transference, it is impossible, finally, to know what is real.

Unfortunately, confusion over what is real and what is transference can hopelessly stall a termination. For instance, if you still think of your therapist as a father, is this a sign that you are still neurotically attached, or that you are simply responding to the very real fatherly cues the entire therapy setup gives you, or both? How do you sort this out? How do you know if it is too soon to go?

Of all the issues that are confronted in therapy, the decision to terminate is often the most bewildering. And to a large degree, many therapists prefer—for good reason—that patients make this decision more or less on their own. For one thing, some therapists feel that the impulse to terminate will be most genuine if it arises entirely from the patient; for another, most therapists do not want to put their patients through the traumatic experience of feeling "dumped" when it is their therapist who initiates a parting instead of them. And, of course, there are those therapists, too, who—as we will see—have their own reasons for prolonging therapy beyond its appropriate end point.

The phenomenon of transference drastically confuses the issue. For example, are you leaving therapy because you always leave important relationships (in which case you need more therapy), or because you have now learned, thanks to therapy, how to stay with important relationships (in which case you don't need more therapy)? Transference means that whatever you—and your therapist—are doing may have transferential motives. At every other point in therapy the presence of these motives is a good thing, because you can use the transference to examine what you are doing in the rest of your life. But with termination therapy *becomes* real life, in the sense that what you are trying to make a decision about is therapy itself, not your job or your lover or your mother. When you attempt to use transference to understand your desire to terminate therapy, you plunge into infinite regress. There is no way to get "outside" the issue, the way therapy normally helps you get outside life issues.

Thus when it comes to termination, psychologizing yourself—closely scrutinizing your motives for wanting to leave, looking for your "true" motives, subjecting yourself to suspicion—is not the answer. All motives are mixed, and the fact that your motives for leaving therapy are mixed, too, is not necessarily a reason to stay.

Instead, the one solid criterion to apply is progress. Are you making progress? Are you changing problematic aspects of your life? This sense of change, of forward motion, is partly but not entirely subjective. Marilyn Ruman, a California clinical psychologist, tells her patients that at the end of therapy two changes will have occurred: their work lives will have improved, and their love lives will have improved. Work and love, the two famous essentials for a fulfilling life. The point is, improvements in these areas are not purely subjective. If you entered therapy hoping to find a steady relationship and now you have, that is an objective change for the better. By the same token, if you entered therapy wanting to change careers and you have done so, that is another objective change for the better. You've done what you wanted to do and there is no reason to stay with therapy simply to "go deeper"—unless profound insight into yourself *is* your goal.

Patients often fear that without their therapists to

prop them up their brave new lives will collapse, and more than one therapist has reinforced this fear in order to hold patients in therapy. But you should respect the positive changes you have made. Real change is hard to change, so to speak.

If you have changed in all or some of the ways you hoped to when you entered therapy, you are right to leave—*even if by staying you might go further yet.* In therapy, there is ultimately no such thing as "all the way." You can always be in therapy; you can always find something new to talk about, or something old that threatens to live and breathe once more. There is no shining moment when suddenly your life becomes fail-safe, when suddenly you are fixed and happy and whole for all time.

If, on the other hand, you haven't achieved your goals but have made discernible movement toward them, you should stay in therapy. You are taking small but worthy steps in life; you are gaining new insight in therapy; things are moving forward. This sense of progress is crucial, because if you are not moving, you are stuck.

Chapter THREE

GETTING
STUCK

Everyone is familiar with marathon therapies, with those people who spend ten, fifteen, twenty years and more faithfully turning up for therapy week after week. Many of these patients are stuck, stalled at a certain juncture in therapy. But you don't have to be in therapy for ten years to be stuck; you could qualify after only a couple of months. You find yourself saying the same things in the same way session after session. There are no new insights, no new attitudes—no progress.

Sometimes this feeling that your therapy has gone stale is simply confirmation that you are finished. You've done what you came to do and now are merely retracing your steps. At other times this immobility is a form of resistance. When you get stuck "accidentally on purpose," you refuse to go any further; you dig in your heels. Furthermore, you can get stuck either for reasons of your own or for reasons of your therapist's—because *you* are doing something wrong, or because *he* is doing something wrong—or both. Finding out the cause is essential to deciding whether you leave or stay and try to work it through.

There are a number of common causes for getting stuck in therapy. Often, a patient will get stuck at a point of intense crisis or conflict. People grind to a halt at such moments because intense crisis and conflict are acutely painful states either to be in or to confront. Getting stuck can be a way out.

Jim, who entered therapy after separating from his wife, stalled for a time over the crisis of his disintegrating marriage. He had left his wife because she was seeing a much older man, and what he wanted most to know was why she had done it. In session after session he tried to talk about her, but his therapist constantly brought the conversation back to Jim, to what had been going on with *him* during the marriage. The upshot was that while Jim had entered therapy feeling like an "innocent victim," he now found himself confronted with an inquiry into his own contribution to his marital failure.

This was hard. "I always felt my therapist was implying that everything was my fault," Jim says today. "If my wife slept with other men, that was because I was too paternal and she needed to rebel—*not* because she had had a miserable relationship with her own father and she was taking it out on me, which was definitely the case. But the thrust of therapy was always to find out about *my* problems, not hers, even though she was loaded with them. It used to make me furious."

Jim balked. For some months he felt extremely angry with his therapist, whom he saw as punitive and judgmental. All progress stopped, and Jim thought seriously about leaving. He had not come to therapy to be blamed.

For Jim, getting stuck was a reason to leave therapy prematurely, a very common experience. For most people the worst aspect of therapy is having to confront what they have contributed to their own problems—a painful process, especially considering how often our problems seem to be visited upon us by others. But finding out what you are "doing wrong" is an unavoidable part of good therapy, and if you leave before you have found out, you have left too soon.

Being asked to accept responsibility for a failed marriage could be enough, in and of itself, to cause a patient to get stuck, but Jim had to face an added blow to his self-esteem. The problem he and his therapist were exploring—namely, his overly paternal attitude toward his wife—was, in fact, an important part of Jim's character. When he went into therapy, Jim was a man who had spent eight years taking care of a profoundly insecure wife who, for her part, eventually began an affair with an even more obvious father figure, an older man with grown children of his own. True, Jim's paternalism was in part a defense: as long as he remained the strong husband in relation to a weak wife, he could avoid seeing how vulnerable he felt as he moved into the adult world of career and family. But paternalism was also a genuine and positive part of his life. He wanted children, and friends and family could always count on him for support. When therapy cast his years of caring for an insecure wife under suspicion, he was profoundly shaken—enough so to get stuck. Fortunately, Jim worked it through and ultimately came away with genuine insight—insight that allowed him to avoid making the same mistakes in his second marriage.

This is often the case with many of our "weaknesses" —they are also our strengths. For example, Linda, a woman in her early thirties whose husband, Eric, had just moved out, went into therapy to try to understand what was happening to her marriage. She had always been cheerful and sunny, while her husband was moody and grim; it was she who maintained a happy atmosphere at home for their three young children. But her capacity to bear up under Eric's temper only seemed to drive him further away, and finally he left, saying he didn't love her.

Linda prided herself on being an optimist, but in therapy this quality quickly came into question. Suddenly her cheery nature began to look like a way of refusing to face up to darker realities—and of refusing to take her husband seriously. Typically, when he was angry she would just keep humming along, essentially ignoring his feelings. When her therapist asked Linda to consider how her unyielding cheer made her husband feel, in retrospect her optimism began to seem positively rude.

At this point Linda got stuck. Finding out that your best quality has helped bring about your downfall is not a pleasant discovery, and Linda was now tempted to leave therapy. Instead she stayed and developed a more complex perception of herself and of how she came across in certain situations. "What I began to see," she says now, "was that Eric just wanted some *response* from me. He wanted me to fight back, to tell him what I was feeling when he went into his rages. When I stayed cheerful it was as if I was rejecting him." This was a valuable insight, especially after Linda and Eric reconciled.

On the other hand, Linda's optimism was, in fact, one of her best qualities—and certainly a necessary one for coping with Eric's mood swings. While Eric calmed down a great deal after their reconciliation and Linda grew more expressive of her own feelings, the truth was that Eric could never head a happy household. Feelings of well-being, so essential to children, had to come from Linda.

•   •   •

When therapy questions personality traits like optimism or paternalism, it can feel like an assault on your most essential characteristics. Whether those characteristics are defenses or strengths—or a combination of both—few patients go into therapy wanting to leave altered beyond recognition. Of course, no one has ever claimed therapy is powerful enough to alter a person beyond recognition. But when you are in therapy, it can seem as if that is what is being asked of you.

Perhaps even more daunting, in therapy your perception of the past also changes. One of the major activities in which therapists and patients engage— and one that causes many patients to stall—is the rewriting of the patient's history. In therapy, you talk about the past. You look to find past patterns in your life, past reasons for those patterns. And in the process, your past changes. The facts, of course, remain the same, but your *beliefs* about the past, your *perceptions*, alter.

Mary's case is typical of such altered perceptions. At thirty-eight she entered therapy because of her love life, which had consisted of three powerful affairs in succession with three men she had worshiped. All three had left her. She mourned each relationship for months—years in one case—before entering into the next one. It was not until the end of the third relationship that she suspected a pattern and sought help.

Thus at the end of her thirties Mary found herself in therapy suddenly discovering that her judgments had been wrong. The men she had given herself to were all raging narcissists—exciting on the surface, glamorous, she had always thought—but hollow when it came to almost everything else. As she worked through her romantic history in therapy, Mary began to acknowledge that none of these men had been particularly good at conversation, nor had they been uniquely adroit in bed.

(At one point she remarked to her therapist that perhaps the reason she had felt so much "chemistry" with one man in particular was that she had never really felt satisfied—hence she was left always feeling enormous desire.) Objectively, none of them lived up to the highly charged image Mary had built up in fantasy.

The real attraction of these men, Mary now saw, had been their unattainability, pure and simple. She had wanted three men she could not have; she had wanted them *because* she could not have them. And she had squandered fifteen years of her life in relationships that were doomed from the start.

Mary's perceptions of her childhood were not faring so well, either. As she and her therapist went on to explore the childhood roots of her choices, she could not help but see that her father—also an adored figure—had been a problematic character as well.

This was a point at which many patients might have fled. As Mary's perceptions of her past changed, she felt herself unmoored. After all, our private histories are an important part of who we are—our pasts *are* our selves, our identities, to an important degree. Our felt identity is built on a lifetime of being the same person, one who *over time* has possessed a more or less coherent set of desires, perceptions, and acts. If we lose that history, we lose our identity, our self. If Mary's history was going to be rewritten, her self was going to be rewritten, too. She would no longer be "Mary who loved not wisely but too well," but "Mary who pursues unattainable men in an unquenchable thirst for approval from her father." She would be a new Mary altogether, and not a welcome one. It was a good moment to leave therapy *forever*.

It is a testament both to Mary's courage and to her therapist's skill that she chose to stay. Mary's case is a good example of what happens when therapy goes well.

Her therapist did not press her to revise her image of herself until she had formed a solid, trusting relationship with him. That way she did not have to feel she was facing these hard facts alone. Moreover, their therapeutic relationship was strong enough by then to weather her impulse to escape, and her therapist engineered their progress in such a fashion that she was not suddenly overwhelmed with awful truth. Over time, Mary modified her perceptions of the past. The pace was slow enough for her to keep up in the present: outside therapy she was beginning to respond to a better breed of man. In this way disillusionment with the past could be coupled with hope for the future.

Thanks largely to her therapist's competence, Mary did not get stuck. Other patients are not so lucky. Therapists can make crucial mistakes—in judgment, tact, timing—that stall their patients' progress. If you are feeling stuck and are considering leaving therapy, you should evaluate not just yourself but your therapist as well before you make that decision. Is *he* doing something that makes you balk?

The most obvious way in which a therapist can stop a patient's progress is to be clumsy or display a lack of tact. Rebecca, a social worker in her late thirties who has been in therapy for nearly twenty years—all her adult life—feels that she spent a good many years stuck in therapy, and for a variety of reasons. But with her most recent (and final) therapist, tactlessness was the cause. Her therapist, also a woman and a social worker, was given to making blunt statements. For example, when Rebecca worried aloud that her brother, an anorexic, might starve to death, her therapist observed that he would be better off dead. She responded with equal sensitivity to another of Rebecca's major concerns, work. Irrationally terrified at the prospect of holding a job, Rebecca had been unemployed for some years. Her therapist's tactless evaluation of this situation: "You're afraid to work because you can't work."

Needless to say, this therapy went nowhere—and took a year and a half to get there. When a therapist gives voice to a patient's worst fears, he forces the patient to put up his guard. Every defense mechanism at the patient's command joins forces with his natural resistance. Change becomes impossible. Rebecca finally recognized this and decided to leave therapy. In this case, it was the right decision.

Therapists may also make more subtle errors in their handling of patients, chiefly due to their own lack of flexibility. For example, a therapist may insist on an interpretation of a patient's behavior that does not work or is simply not true, despite the fact that all the textbooks and the therapist's training suggest that it *is* true. Suppose a therapist tells a patient who has trouble holding jobs that the cause is unresolved anger toward his father. Suppose, too, that this interpretation makes no sense whatsoever to the patient. Perhaps the real reason behind his trouble keeping a job is his extreme terror of exposure—a fear that when his colleagues see his work, they will condemn him as a fraud.

The patient can do one of three things in such a situation. He can disagree outright, in which case he and his therapist lock horns and go no further. Or he can agree outwardly while disagreeing inwardly, in which case again therapy comes to a halt, because the patient no longer completely trusts his therapist. Or the patient can try to talk himself into his therapist's interpretation, on grounds that the therapist is the expert and must know what he's talking about. Here, too, the patient will end up becoming stuck, because he is trying to believe something that simply does not fit. Any apparent progress from here on is built on a wrong premise, and thus is not real progress at all.

In short, if your therapist is completely inflexible and insists on interpretations you absolutely cannot buy, your therapy is in trouble. Worse, your therapy can be in trouble even if your therapist is *right*, but his timing is wrong. If your therapist moves too fast, even if his analyses are correct you may end up stuck.

Maria experienced this in her therapy. At twenty-four she had graduated from college but was still living at home, very much attached to her mother. She could not seem to get her life going. She wanted to apply to graduate school but was not doing so; she wanted to work but was not applying for jobs. On the love front, she was drawn exclusively to adventurers, men who were utterly irresponsible in their dealings with women. Maria's sexual problems formed a perfect fit with her other problems, especially those in her relationship with her mother. Still a daughter first and foremost, she was drawn only to men who did not challenge this identity in any serious way. A man who might have asked her to marry him would have been a man trying to wrench her away from home. Maria needed to see this connection between her seemingly disparate problems.

Finally she moved away from home and began to see a therapist, but her therapy did not go well. For one thing, she developed a crush on her therapist, who was the first man of his type—articulate, responsible, solid —with whom she had had much contact. Her own parents were divorced, and her father had moved to another state.

Suddenly one day a wedding band appeared on her therapist's finger. Maria was crushed. When she asked him about the ring, he said he had been married all along. This was bad enough, but then, in the natural course of events, some months later he announced that he and his wife were expecting a baby. After dropping this second bombshell (Maria had never entirely recovered from the discovery that he was married), he asked Maria how she felt. She said "all the right things," offering congratulations and so on, and he did not question her further.

But soon after, his behavior changed significantly. "To me it seemed as if the closer he came to being a father in his own life, the more he tried to be a father in my life, too," says Maria. He began to press her to make changes, to apply to graduate school, find a better job, buy a car—get her life together. He pursued these topics with such alacrity that Maria began to feel more and more anxious at the prospect of each session. Therapy was throwing her into terrible distress.

Maria's was a case of a therapist pushing things much too fast. By now Maria was living in a beach house with several roommates, swimming, going to parties, writing poetry. She was learning to be happy among her own peers, she was independent, she was making progress. But her therapist was impatient. Beach life, to him, was no life at all; he wanted her launched on a career path, and the sooner the better. She was postponing her life, he said.

Increasingly anxious and resentful, Maria resisted. Progress soon stopped, though the actual end of her therapy did not arrive for some months more. Finally, after dropping in and out a few times, she told her therapist she could not see him anymore because therapy was causing her such severe anxiety. When she asked him why she should be feeling so bad he answered that she wasn't "working hard enough," thus laying the blame squarely on her shoulders. That was the end of her therapy.

Bad timing was at least partially responsible. Maria did plan to apply to graduate school, find a better job, and buy a car—*ultimately*—but she could only do all these things according to her own schedule. When her therapist tried to impose his timetable on her, Maria first became stuck, then finally left.

Judging by the sequence of events in Maria's therapy, we can surmise that a powerful countertransference was probably interfering with treatment. Becoming a father in his own life appears to have altered this therapist's approach to his young client. He may well have begun to take her "failings" personally, the way a parent reacts to his own child's problems. Now, instead of acting as a therapist, he had assumed the role of a standard-setting, judgmental—and probably very worried—dad, a dad exhorting his wayward daughter to pull herself together.

The point is, a therapist's countertransference can derail your therapy. If you appear to be stuck in your own therapy, consider whether you and your therapist may have fallen into stereotyped roles *other* than those of patient/client. A countertransference is usually a dyad, a set of two roles or types that fit together: father/daughter, man/woman, boss/employee, and so on. Each therapist's form of countertransference is individual, of course: father/daughter for one therapist would be quite different from father/daughter for another. But if you feel, as Maria did, that a strong father/daughter interaction is structuring your sessions with your therapist, this can be—and probably is—the reason you are feeling stuck.

More subtle, a particular countertransference can be unique to your particular therapist. Say a therapist has always felt insecure about his capacity to speak well; he thinks of himself as a better listener than talker, and he has always felt insecure around highly articulate people. It is easy to see what can go wrong when a trial lawyer—a person who makes his living from persuasive and fluent speech—shows up in this therapist's office seeking therapy. All the therapist's insecurities about speech are likely to be mobilized, and the therapist may be tempted simply to listen silently to the eloquent patient before him. For his part, the lawyer may be happy to fill his entire fifty-minute hour "arguing his case" with no response from the opposition—which may be part of his problem. Therapist and patient would be forming a perfect fit, but not a productive one.

On the other hand, an alert therapist would examine his own reactions for clues as to how this patient was affecting others in his life. And as therapy progressed, the therapist's countertransference would probably change. As an example of this process, Jerrold Maxmen, M.D., author of *The New Psychiatry*, offers an anecdote about a psychiatrist who was seeing a high-powered female attorney who typically behaved like a daughter when she was with him. Naturally his countertransference made him feel like her father. But as therapy progressed, she changed; she began to behave more like an adult. One night the psychiatrist dreamed that a teenager, dressed like this patient, came to therapy and sat on his lap, then got up and walked away. Interpreting his dream, he realized that while his patient had changed, he had not. He was still treating her like a daughter. After this he changed, too. He began to position her as the grown woman she was, thereby using his countertransference sensitively and productively.

When it becomes a problem, the countertransference issue means that there are certain topics that your therapist simply cannot handle. Often, patients sense this and begin to censor themselves, consciously or not. If you are stuck because you are consistently withholding certain information or feelings from your therapist, you may have gone as far as you can go with this therapist.

Looking back over her twenty years in therapy, Rebecca finally saw that all of her therapists had had one area about which they simply could not speak. Her first therapist, who ultimately ended Rebecca's therapy with a confession of desire for her, could not talk about sex (a particularly astonishing gap since Rebecca was an unwed pregnant teenager at the time). Her second therapist, whose father had committed suicide, could not talk about Rebecca's suicidal feelings. Her third therapist, who owned a fleet of six sports cars, could not talk about her compulsive spending. In each case, the therapist balked at the material closest to his or her own difficulties.

It is a commonplace among therapists that the patient can go no further than the therapist. Patients must take this wisdom to heart. Therapists are people, too, and they have their areas of vulnerability—areas they will not deal with well, if at all, in their patients' therapy. If you are stuck because your therapist simply cannot address a major topic in your life, this is reason enough to leave.

Countertransference aside, there are times when the patient may be bringing in material the therapist simply does not relate to. A young therapist dealing with a sixty-year-old's fear of death, a childless therapist dealing with a mother's guilt over working—these may not be the most productive matches between therapist and patient. Good therapy demands empathy, and all of us empathize better with people whose problems we have experienced or anticipate experiencing.

A therapy mismatch can produce a stall. Karen discovered this after *fifteen years* of therapy, a stint that ended only when her therapist committed suicide.

These had not been fifteen years of onward and upward progress; Karen had been treading water for a very long time. True, therapy had helped her enormously with her work life, but her love life was far from happy. Worse, it was unhappy in the exact same way it had been when she first entered therapy fifteen years before.

Now her therapist was gone. His loss was painful enough, but the revelations that followed—of his homosexual relationships with male patients—were more shattering yet. Abruptly Karen saw all too clearly why she had been stuck. Her major problems had had to do with her sexuality, and her psychiatrist had simply not been able to deal with her as a heterosexual woman. (This is not to say that *no* homosexual therapist can treat a heterosexual client. But in Karen's case, her therapist had major problems with sexuality, even to the degree that he had violated the prohibition against therapist-client sexual relations with his male patients.) He could do wonders with Karen's childhood, wonders with her career issues, but he was consistently off base in any discussion of her love life.

"He actively encouraged me to marry my husband," Karen remembers now, "a man who anyone could have seen was wrong for me." Her husband was emotionally and physically abusive, and the marriage ended after a year. "The other thing was that he never made me look at my love life," Karen says, "at what I was really doing. Instead he would make excuses. 'It's hard to meet the right person,' he would say." So hard, in his view, that marrying an abusive man in order to be married to *somebody* made sense to him.

Clearly, he was not responding to her sexual dilemma with any degree of real perception or insight. For her part, while Karen had long sensed that something was askew, she could not quite bring herself to recognize the truth. And she did not want to confront her psychiatrist about her frustration—she feared hurting his feelings. She wanted to protect him. Because she was holding things back in order to avoid wounding her psychiatrist, Karen was stuck.

Any time you *persistently* feel protective of your therapist you should wonder what is going on. Most patients feel protective toward their therapists at some point. Few of us want to hurt people we care about, and patients often care about their therapists. But the point of therapy is to "work through" this phase. If you stop at protectiveness, you stop the course of therapy.

Protectiveness prevents any expression of anger. Karen never questioned her therapist's attitudes and never felt angry toward him. They were on good terms for fifteen years, with each session pitched at the same soothing tone. Her therapy was pleasant and supportive, but unemotional, and strong emotions are necessarily involved in working through long-standing conflicts.

The professional term for Karen's situation is "collusion": therapist and patient collude to keep certain truths at bay. Karen picked up on semiconscious signals from her therapist, he picked up on semiconscious signals from her, and both tacitly agreed to leave sex out of their discussions.

Karen's mistake lay in trying to shield her therapist from any criticism of his work. However, her motives were not entirely altruistic; in protecting her therapist, she was also protecting herself. When her therapist could not deal with her sexual problems, she did not confront him with this fact. If she had, she would have been forced to see that she was on her own—that he could not help her any more than he already had.

It is not uncommon for patient and therapist to collude in order to avoid the rebellious midsection of therapy, with its attendant angers and hurts. The patient enters therapy admiring his therapist, and in this case continues to admire him unreservedly for *years*. The patient probably feels better whenever they meet. Little changes in the rest of his life, but he feels good during therapy itself. In other words, patient and therapist have made an unconscious agreement to avoid exploring bad feelings toward the therapist. The patient stays put in the initial, "adoration" phase of therapy.

The trouble is, while adoration is much more comfortable for therapist and patient both, it does not help the patient learn that relationships can weather bad feelings. If you have been in therapy for more than a few months without ever feeling anything other than affection toward your therapist, you should suspect that you may be colluding with him to avoid more challenging topics. And you should bring this up in therapy.

Therapists must, of course, make it possible for patients to express criticisms of their treatment. Many, many patients report keeping their dissatisfactions to themselves in order to avoid hurting their therapist's feelings—or to stay in their good graces, which is an entirely rational reason for keeping your complaints to yourself. More than one survey has shown that therapists like best those patients who make them feel like *good* therapists. In other words, they like patients who seem to be getting better; in particular, they like patients who seem to be getting better *because* of therapy. If you come in with complaints that you are *not* getting better, you do, in fact, risk losing some of your therapist's affection, at least for that session.

Giving criticism is difficult in any situation, but there are additional obstacles structured into the therapeutic setup. The limited time you spend in therapy works against the free flow of criticism. It is easy enough to keep your irritation to yourself for a mere fifty minutes; in fact, you may well fear that if you do express criticism you won't have enough time to patch things up afterward. Anger is intrinsically distancing, and people usually recover from hostile criticism by spending a great deal of "normal" time together after an argument has ended. This is not possible in therapy, where you may have to wait several days before seeing your therapist again. A patient given to worry (Did I go too far? Have I alienated my therapist for good?) may well find these intervening days too troublesome to be worth the effort of expressing dissatisfaction. Also, of course, the fact that you never know what your therapist thinks works against being open about your criticism. Not being able to read your therapist's response may make the prospect of voicing criticism and then *imagining* what he is feeling simply too daunting.

A good therapist will question his patients about any bad feelings they may have toward him. He will usually know when you may be feeling angry, and he will often have an idea about why. As a professional he knows that certain situations almost invariably irk patients, such as when the therapist changes (or misses) an appointment. When this happens a skilled therapist will ask his patient whether he has any reactions to the changed or missed appointment. Moreover, a therapist should be very good at picking up on the unspoken. Body language, significant looks, not smiling—all these are clues that the patient may be disgruntled. In particular, any time a normally talkative patient arrives at a session with nothing to say, his therapist should be alerted to the possible presence of bad feelings. It is up to the therapist to make the patient feel that he is welcome to articulate criticisms.

Hans Strupp offers a telling example of a therapist

soliciting a patient's negative feelings, then putting them to good use in therapy. A patient whose fundamental problem was her "inability to constructively assert herself and express anger" had progressed in her therapy to the point of being able to openly express her sexual feelings for her therapist. The therapist did not handle these revelations, which had been difficult for her to make, with as much sensitivity as he might have. Rather bluntly he chalked them up to his patient's desire to take revenge on her husband, in essence telling her that she didn't *really* feel what she thought she felt: she didn't truly desire him, she was just getting even with her mate. Essentially he discounted her emotions. She responded with real—though unfocused—anger. Two sessions later she arrived complaining of a persistent headache; she had had a frustrating and irritable couple of days all told. Wisely, the therapist did not let this go by.

The transcript of the subsequent session shows how a seasoned therapist handles such a sign of bad feeling. By way of broaching the subject, he asked his patient whether there was anything else besides the various immediate problems of the past few days that was adding to her "pain in the head." Given this sincere invitation to air her grievances, she readily confessed that she had been "feeling really low from the previous session." She went on to say that his reaction to her sexual desire had made her feel "foolish and ridiculous."

Responding with the honesty and integrity that are the hallmarks of a professional, her therapist first acknowledged his own role in making his patient feel that way. "Whatever part I contributed," he said, "is something that I need to look at." He then moved her forward to consider how this sequence of events mirrored her relationship with her mother: for years her efforts to get closer to her mother had been met with continual rebuffs. The patient readily saw the parallel; in this case, the move to get closer to her therapist (by expressing sexual desire) had brought her more rejection when he told her that sexual desire for him wasn't really what she felt.

This is good therapy. The therapist invited expression of negative feeling and rewarded that expression with empathy, understanding, and a ready willingness to acknowledge whatever role he himself had played in provoking such feeling. In short, the good therapist uses moments like these to move therapy forward, to make progress.

Another essential attribute of a good therapist is the capacity to instill hope that things, that the patient, can *change*. This quality may be more rare among therapists than one would think. When I interviewed a group of therapists on the subject of change, I found that most of them believed personal change to be a profoundly difficult and infrequent occurrence. One therapist actually grew despondent during the interview, remarking after a time, "This is a depressing topic." Several said the goal of therapy was not change but simply self-acceptance (which is, to be fair, one kind of change). While self-acceptance may be a goal of any therapy, the obvious problem with this line of thinking is: What if your particular self can't hold a job or can't stay with a relationship? Do you need to spend upwards of a hundred dollars a week to *accept* this state of affairs?

To instill hope, a therapist must be careful not to focus too exclusively on the negative—an exceedingly delicate task considering that therapy's mandate is to address the patient's troubles. One of the unspoken rules of therapy is that you talk about your problems. You don't talk about the weather, you don't talk about politics, you don't talk about a great movie you just saw. Of course, no therapist ever explicitly lays down these rules, and in fact many patients do come to therapy and talk about the weather, politics, movies. But when they do, their therapists go on the alert. During his professional training, the therapist is taught to encourage the patient to consider why he is wasting valuable therapy time on such topics—and the answer is likely to be that the patient is resisting therapy.

Should the patient bring in good news, therapy's unspoken insistence on the negative can quickly turn into the proverbial rain on the parade. Hilary became acutely aware of this phenomenon during her three years in therapy. "When I first went in," she says, "I was job-hunting and miserable. I had no self-esteem, and we spent a lot of time talking about how my parents had felt like failures in their own lives, and how I had absorbed this self-concept from them." This insight helped Hilary continue to look for work in spite of feeling so low, because she could set aside her feelings of worthlessness and press on with the search. She still *felt* bad, but because therapy was showing her low self-esteem to be a childhood leftover, she was able to *act* as if she had some faith. Eventually, she landed a good management trainee position at a New York bank.

After that her career took off. She received a promotion within six months, then another a year or so later. But to her surprise she found that therapy was somewhat less helpful when it came to celebrating success. "Basically I was just feeling great from all these promotions—especially since they were so beyond my wildest expectations, given the family I had grown up in. But I would go to therapy all thrilled to report my new good news, and I'd come away feeling crummy again."

Therapy, she felt, was deflating her happiness. "I'd

tell my therapist the news, and he would be really warm and congratulate me. Then there would be a few moments while I sort of filled him in—when it happened, what they said when they told me, that kind of thing. Then there'd be a pause and he would say, 'So how are you feeling about all this?' or 'So you're feeling good about yourself today.' Somehow, that moment just seemed to be my cue to switch into doom."

Hilary would then start to investigate her "deeper" feelings about success. And, not surprisingly, those deeper feelings proved to be darker as well—after all, she had already revealed all her happy feelings about the promotion; there were no more positive emotions left to report. By the end of a session, she would have wondered aloud whether her parents and friends would reject her for her success, whether she would do something to sabotage herself in order to remain within the family fold, whether her success at work masked a serious failure at love, and so on. None of these disturbing possibilities had occurred to her in her moment of triumph; they came to her only in her moment of therapeutic reflection. She would leave therapy feeling down.

She would also leave feeling restless, with the sense that it was time to "graduate." In truth, it probably was time, but by the end of a session Hilary felt like such a troubled person she could not justify making the break. She was stuck.

You might be inclined to believe that Hilary, coming from a family in which both parents considered themselves life's losers, did in fact harbor a potentially destructive ambivalence toward success—and that getting in touch with this ambivalence would be essential to resolving it. But before making this assumption consider again the unspoken rules of therapy and the therapeutic culture that surrounds it. For Freud, the unconscious is by definition deep and dark. The unconscious consists entirely of *repressed* feelings, images, wishes—repressed because they threaten the conscious ego. Sunny, nonthreatening feelings, images, and wishes have no need for repression and so can be experienced consciously.

Few ideas of Freud's have been more thoroughly assimilated into popular thinking than the principle that the unconscious is essentially negative. In his book *Civilization and Its Discontents* he argued that civilization depends on "sublimations" of unacceptable infantile impulses. An artist, for example, might be sublimating a desire to play with feces; a surgeon might be sublimating powerful aggressive impulses. This is the stuff of which classic Freudian analysis is made.

These days psychologists are considerably more genteel in their perceptions of the unconscious—hardly anyone talks about the child's desire to play with feces anymore. But the principle of the negative unconscious still holds: "behind" an individual artist's impulse to create might be, for example, a grandstanding grab for the attention he or she did not receive as a child. That is why you find patients like Jim having his paternalism analyzed as an unconscious attempt to be invulnerable, or Linda having her optimism interpreted as a form of emotional withdrawal. These days it is hard to believe in an unmixed motive, and it is impossible when you are talking to your therapist. Simple happiness—unalloyed joy—is a thing of the distant, eighteenth-century past.

In short, Hilary's problem may not have been fear of success. Her trouble by this point in her therapy may simply have been that she is living in the twentieth century, in a *therapeutic culture.* Her therapist did not tell her that every happy feeling had to have its corresponding bad feeling; he did not have to. Hilary herself had probably read enough popular psychology to have developed the conviction that a cigar is never just a cigar. Her therapy situation was "overdetermined," to borrow another compelling term from Freud, which means that a number of factors combined to rob her of her triumph—to snatch defeat from the jaws of victory, so to speak. Up until then her therapy had only been about problems; whenever her therapist asked what she was feeling she had responded with a *negative* feeling, and she had always understood therapy—anybody's therapy—to be exclusively about one's troubles in life. All these factors added up to a powerful if unspoken demand that Hilary look on the dark side. When she did, she seemed to find ample confirmation that things were not so rosy as she might have supposed, and she could not summon up the optimism to leave therapy.

A better therapist would have conducted Hilary's therapy rather differently. For one thing, he or she would have fostered an atmosphere in which Hilary felt able to complain openly about the pessimistic tone of her sessions, instead of keeping her discontent to herself. For another, he would have been monitoring the good-news-bad-feeling sequence the two of them had fallen into. He would have spotted this pattern, thought about it, possibly brought it up in session. He would have done his best to figure out what part of it was coming from Hilary and what part from him. If he discovered that he was reinforcing bad news more than good—through expressions of interest, sympathy, and the like—he would have changed.

Unfortunately, choosing a therapist who inspires hope is not a simple matter of finding someone who radiates enthusiasm. Therapy is not cheerleading, although therapist-cheerleaders abound—particularly on the

West Coast, where inspirational psychotherapy organizations have flourished. A sample motto of one such group: "If you can't afford to join our group, you can't afford not to."

Bill, at twenty-three one of the youngest executives in Hollywood, was seeing a therapist whose upbeat supportiveness hindered more than helped. Just out of school, Bill lived in a state of ongoing, frenzied suspense about his job. As a development executive for a production company, his role was to find projects for his company to produce, then sell them to a studio. Since each studio considers thousands of projects a year—and puts only 150 or so into development—all production companies are up against fierce competition with each project they bring in.

Constantly on the line and waiting to hear if his latest project had been accepted or rejected, Bill found himself unable to read scripts. He excelled at meetings and negotiations, but he simply could not read the fifteen or more scripts he needed to get through each week. He was blocked, which posed a real danger to his career for obvious reasons. He was not high enough in the ranks to be able to rely on someone else to do his reading for him, and if you can't read you can't search effectively for new material. Nor can you offer suggestions for where to go with the characters and story lines of the properties you have already bought. Bill was turning up at story conferences not having read the most recent draft of a script his company was developing.

Bill needed help. Instead, what he got from his therapist was a rationalization for his problem: Bill, his therapist said, could not read scripts because he was a genius. His IQ was too high for him to be able to do the repetitive work of script reading. He needed mental stimulation and change.

Bill's therapist specialized in Hollywood clients, and it is not hard to see why. When you are locked into a business as competitive as the television and film industry, it is not entirely a bad thing to have your therapist tell you that your only problem is you are a genius. But being told you are a genius is not therapy. Even a genius needs to do his job if he wants to keep it, and Bill did not break through his block as a result of therapy. In fact, he felt that if anything his therapist was actually reinforcing his problem by complimenting him for having it. He was stuck.

The most overriding error that even the most able of therapists can make is simply not recognizing a good therapeutic outcome when he sees it. An otherwise excellent therapist might fail to perceive the extent of your improvement because little in his years of training has taught him *how* to perceive improvement. Robert S. Wallerstein, M.D., author of *Forty-Two Lives in Treatment*, a long-term study of treatment outcomes for forty-two patients at the Menninger Foundation, discusses this dilemma at length. According to Wallerstein, while therapists have developed a sophisticated set of criteria for identifying and characterizing mental illness, they do not possess an adequate set of criteria either for identifying "ideal mental health" (usually called "positive mental health" in the literature) or for measuring the degree of progress a patient has made. In short, therapists are underschooled when it comes to knowing what it looks like when a patient gets better.

You can see this clearly when you read professional writings: the vocabulary for discussing emotional problems is rich, elaborate, sophisticated. But look for descriptions of emotional health in the same texts and you find very little. The popular press has given us vague allusions to "self-actualization" and the like, but such positive concepts have not attracted wide attention among theorists. Instead, scholars devote their major energies to developing the more negatively tinged constructs—constructs such as "narcissism," to cite one notable example—related to mental health.

This inclination should not be surprising, given Freud's view of mental health, which was that, essentially, health is simply a lesser form of neurosis:

> But a normal ego...is, like normality in general, an ideal fiction. The abnormal ego...is unfortunately no fiction. Every normal person, in fact, is only normal on the average. His ego approximates to that of the psychotic in some part or other and to a greater or lesser extent....

This belief, of course, makes therapy a highly paradoxical enterprise—one of the "impossible professions," as Freud himself put it. People go into therapy to be made well when, according to psychoanalysis, there is no such animal as the truly well—in the sense of truly normal—human being. Only the abnormal is real.

Of course, most therapists—and many patients—experience this same line of thought as highly liberating, and in a way it is. Once you see every man, woman, and child as more or less neurotic, you are released from the pressure to make yourself perfect in human relations: ambivalence, fear, hostility—all of the "negative" emotions—become entirely acceptable states.

But when it comes to therapy this blurring of the normal with the abnormal can work against the patient. Consider Freud's language: a "normal ego" is a "fiction." It *does not exist.* If your therapist adheres to this belief system, as his patient you have to ask yourself what it may be doing to his capacity to perceive wellness. Quite possibly it has left him with a blind spot; when a therapist believes that normalcy does not exist (except as a reassuring fiction), he will automatically look for the "dark side" and hidden conflicts in anyone who appears actually to be normal. This means that no matter how much progress you make, your therapist is still going to perceive remaining conflicts and potentially dangerous problems.

Depending on the personality of the therapist, this perception can work to the good or the ill of the patient. An essentially optimistic, noncritical therapist will tend to take a "good enough is good enough" attitude, sending much-improved patients on their way. One useful formulation of this approach is that of Los Angeles psychologist Marilyn Ruman, who observes that no one ever becomes a "transcendent being." The end of therapy, for her, arrives when a patient can "do the work of therapy on his own"—a logical, and functional, resolution of the basic Freudian paradox. On the other hand, there is also the therapist who is highly perfectionist *on his patient's behalf.* For this therapist good enough is most adamantly *not* good enough, and he does not issue bills of health because he never feels that his work is done. Refusing to settle for anything less than perfection, this therapist may never let go.

Even the very best of therapists can make crucial errors in judgment and perception, which means that if you are stalled in therapy, you must try to find out why in order to make an informed judgment about whether to leave or to stay. The first line of action is to discuss your apparent lack of progress honestly with your therapist. You owe that much to yourself. He probably feels the same way, and may have a good explanation. If his feeling, in so many words, is that you are resisting treatment, take him seriously. A major clue here is any feelings of defensiveness you may have. If you feel as if you are being "blamed" for your problems, if you believe that your therapist thinks your troubles are your own fault, this may be a sign that you *are* in fact resisting therapy. You may want to stay with it for a time longer.

On the other hand, if the problem is coming from your therapist, he may be able to see this, too. While many therapists have a policy against admitting mistakes, many others believe in owning up when they have misstepped. If your therapist suggests he may have been pushing too hard—or stating interpretations too bluntly, or any of the various mistakes discussed above—again, this is reason to stay. He will change his tack, and progress can resume.

Finally, if your therapist does not see *any* contribution he is making to your lack of progress, and if he does not give *any* convincing assessment as to what contribution you are making, you have to consider the possibility that he is not doing his job as well as he should. Again, ask yourself whether you are holding anything back in deference to your therapist's feelings. Any time you find yourself not telling your therapist things you think will hurt, offend, or draw a blank, this is a danger sign—especially if you have ventured into these areas before without success. You are probably picking up signals that these are subjects with which your therapist prefers, for whatever reason, not to deal. If you are deliberately withholding criticisms in order to protect him, this, too, is trouble. You need to level with him and see what happens. If your therapy changes for the better, staying with it is probably the right move.

If it doesn't change, you may have gone as far as you can go with this therapist. Or you may have gone as far as you can—or should—go with *any* therapist. The principle to remember is that therapy is going well when it is *going,* when you have a sense of progress, when you feel encouraged to say what's on your mind. Life, work, and love should be coming to seem less brittle occupations. Things seem possible.

Chapter FOUR

TIES THAT BIND: LOVING YOUR THERAPIST

Nicole has now been in therapy, attending sessions four times weekly, for eight years. Although she is herself a clinical psychologist, she tells friends seriously that she is "in love" with Dr. Bernstein, that he is "the perfect man." At thirty-eight she is eager to marry and have a child, but none of the men she meets measures up to her doctor.

Eight years ago, just turning thirty, she went into therapy to find help with her love life; now therapy *is* her love life. Dr. Bernstein, a man who has been married to another woman for thirty years, has come to fill the "significant other" place in Nicole's heart and mind. Psychologically speaking, he is her mate, even though she is not his. This psychic reality makes leaving therapy, for Nicole, tantamount to divorce. As a result, she has no intention of leaving; she will turn forty in analysis with no end in sight, and no family of her own.

From her friends' point of view, the intensity of Nicole's longing is unfathomable. She is a dynamic and sexy woman who rarely lacks for dates. Dr. Bernstein is twenty years her senior, short, somewhat paunchy, and entirely bald. He is reserved and monotone in manner, married, with children in college. If Nicole had met her therapist at a party, her friends agree, she would have moved on long ago—if she had had anything to do with him in the first place.

Critics of psychotherapy often see the therapist as little more than a glorified rent-a-friend. In fact, though, a patient's relationship with his therapist is more intense than most friendships: rent-a-lover might be more apropros. Most patients have the occasional erotic dream about their therapists (even when the therapist is of the same sex) without the therapist's doing anything unprofessional to spark such imagery. And while everyone knows how destructive it is to sleep with your therapist, few patients have considered the potential dangers involved in merely fantasizing about him or her.

Moreover, the structure of therapy encourages such fantasizing—on both sides. A study done by clinical psychologist Kenneth S. Pope found that 87 percent of psychologists (95 percent of the men and 76 percent of the women) reported having been sexually attracted to their patients on occasion. By rights, these figures should not have come as the surprise they did when Pope's survey first appeared. In the classic formulation of psychoanalyst Phyllis Greenacre, "If two people are repeatedly alone together, some sort of emotional bond will develop between them." Greenacre was speaking of the transference, but her observation applies equally well to the kindling of desire. This is the phenomenon of people growing attracted to each other when fate throws them together under circumstances both intense and intimate. Campus mates sharing a ride cross-country, camp counselors working and bunking together over the summer, actors working on location

—all of these situations generate sparks between people who in any other situation would be merely passing acquaintances.

Therapy, too, is an intense and intimate experience that brings together two people who under other circumstances might not even notice one another. In fact, therapy by nature is so intense and intimate that it would be surprising if therapists did *not* react. (Some therapists recognize this reality. Strupp cites the case of a male therapist who, puzzled at finding himself unattracted to a particular female patient, examines his lack of reaction for clues as to what is happening in the therapy.) In short, within the confines of an entirely professional, platonic therapeutic relationship—and a full 93.5 percent of Pope's therapists had never acted upon their feelings—a sexual bond may still develop. And sexual bonds can be powerful indeed.

Here we come to one of the thorniest issues you face in deciding whether, and when, to leave therapy: the very real possibility that you have fallen in love with your therapist, wittingly or not. When your therapist is a powerful presence in your life—powerful through his unconditional there-ness, his link with painful relationships of the past, his stature and authority—you have to ask yourself whether your attachment to him is helping or hurting your attachments to others. How is therapy affecting your love life?

Interviews with unmarried patients like Nicole suggest that a much-loved therapist can indeed jeopardize a patient's ability to function in the dating world. Like Nicole, a patient can end up in love with a forever-unattainable therapist. Moreover, you can fall in love even if you don't fantasize sexual relations with your therapist, even if you don't *think* of yourself as infatuated.

Joanna's experience poignantly illustrates that this

phenomenon is not limited to unmarried women, or to patients and therapists of the opposite sex. At forty-five, she was struggling with overwhelming problems. Her husband had lost his job, her son had developed Tourette's disease, and she had ruptured two disks in her spine. This last misfortune had resulted in chronic back pain so fierce she could not leave her bed. There she lay, crushed under a load of constant physical and psychic pain. Her husband and children resented her plight; she was not functioning as the reliable wife and mother she had always been, and instead of being sympathetic, they were angry and removed. Feeling overpowered by her troubles, Joanna went into therapy.

Her therapist was a younger woman who was caring and empathetic. Joanna had begun to write poetry; her therapist read all her poems. Joanna wanted to apply to a graduate program in poetry writing; her therapist encouraged her. She was there for Joanna in all the ways her family was not and Joanna responded accordingly. She grew more and more attached to her therapist, writing her letters in between sessions. She thought about her constantly; she imagined long conversations with her, heartfelt exchanges, and affection.

Essentially, Joanna had fallen in love. Hers was a schoolgirl crush—the kind young girls can get on a favorite female teacher. Joanna admired and looked up to her therapist, and wanted her therapist to admire her back. Although she did not imagine sexual relations with her therapist, she was completely enraptured nonetheless.

Meanwhile, little had improved at home. This is the real danger in becoming too bound up with a therapist: therapy can become merely an escape from harsh realities, rather than the means of facing up to them. Your therapist ceases to be a therapist and becomes the wished-for perfect lover, friend, spouse, parent. You content yourself with therapy and therapist, and stop trying in the world at large—possibly without even knowing you have given up.

Of course, there still remains the chicken-and-egg question: which came first? Did Joanna use therapy to turn away from her family, or did she go into therapy because her family had turned away from her? Even in so seemingly clear-cut a case as Nicole's, you have to ask if Nicole is closed off emotionally to other men because she is in love with her therapist, or if she is in love with her therapist because she is closed off. Is her therapy-love a result of poor therapy or a symptom of emotional makeup? Or are both propositions true?

While sorting out cause and effect is close to impossible, Nicole's case seems relatively simple. Something is not right with her therapy. At the very least, her infatuation should be an ongoing topic in her therapy. Her therapist should be subtly and tactfully positioning his patient's fixation on him as a *problem*. Because he does not do this, she takes his silence on the subject as tacit acceptance of her love. Her devotion to him is simply a given of their relationship; since they do not talk about her love for him, it "goes without saying." Partly, of course, Nicole *wants* to think her doctor welcomes her love—but the point is, her doctor is doing nothing to discourage her in this belief. And that is his responsibility.

Other cases are more subtle. Thirty-two years old now, Jeff has been seeing his female therapist since the age of twenty-five. During that time he has slept with scores—possibly hundreds—of women. He wants, he says, to fall in love, marry, and have children, but he cannot bring it off. The one year-long steady relationship he did manage to sustain during this period finally succumbed to his daily inability to make up his mind: did he love this woman enough? Ultimately the answer was no.

Naturally he discusses his love life with his therapist weekly. She is the one emotional constant in his life, the only woman with whom he has remained steadily involved over the years. However, he is not in love with her. He speaks coolly of her; she is intelligent, he believes, though not a "major intellect." He does not fantasize about her. She does, however, remind him "slightly" of the one lost love of his life. During his law school days, Jeff fell passionately in love with an older, professionally established woman who utterly devastated him. His therapist, also a professionally established older woman, calls this first love to mind.

Of course, this kind of transference is what is supposed to happen; Jeff *should* transfer this ruinous older woman of the past onto the older woman of the present. But *seven years* of transference with no end in sight? Jeff is not getting any younger, and his goals are not getting any closer. While men do not face a biological clock, the women they marry do. Since Jeff is attracted to older women, he is fast reaching the point at which having children with a woman he loves will become an iffy proposition.

Thus, Jeff's is a case where a transference may be doing more harm than good. Involved with his therapist, Jeff is not really available. He dates constantly, he sleeps around, but he always reports back to his therapist. She is mother and lover in one, a surrogate spouse. On the other hand, whether or not his therapist is responsible for this situation is an open question. From the outside Jeff looks like a person who has never gotten over an early loss, and we might surmise that therapy is simply his defense against falling too hard again. He has plugged his therapist into his personal scenario and is using her as a shield against "real" women out in the real world. If he did not have therapy he would have some other means of protection.

The real issue in Jeff's case, as in Nicole's, is not whether therapy is *causing* his problems, but whether therapy is doing anything significant to *end* them, or whether it has stopped being therapy and has become part of a private scenario. The well-known political saying that one is either part of the solution or part of the problem may well hold true here. Therapy that is not—or is no longer—helping your life may have begun to hurt your life. Transforming their therapists into surrogate spouses, Jeff and Nicole may be using therapy to avoid change.

While Nicole's rather dramatic situation is relatively rare, many patients find themselves in Jeff's position. They have been seeing the same therapist for years, and their love lives never quite jell. Perhaps they do not form long-term relationships; perhaps they do manage a long-term involvement but it's on-again off-again; perhaps they date one person steadily for years but can't get over the marriage hump even though they say they want to. At heart these people cannot commit. The longest, most enduring relationship of their adult lives is the one they are having with their therapist. Whatever their problems going in, these patients are now so entrenched with their therapists that there is little emotional room left for anyone new.

In most cases therapy or the therapist is not strictly to "blame" for these situations, but there are times when an individual therapist does help the process along. Certain words and statements lend themselves to romantic interpretation and encourage the patient to harbor hope. For instance, one woman who was very much in love with her therapist felt that he was implicitly confessing erotic feelings of his own when he observed that he and she had "chemistry." Possibly he was referring to the easy rapport they had developed in their sessions, but in the culture at large, "chemistry," when used to characterize a male-female relationship, means sexual appeal. For him to use the term without specifying precisely what he meant was irresponsible.

While it is often difficult to sort out therapy's effects on those who cannot sustain a commitment in real life —or those whose real-life commitments are troubled— the potentially negative impact of individual therapy on an already existing, committed relationship is clear. There is no doubt that therapy can come between mates. Freud himself knew this. When his former patient Helene Deutsch (who would herself become a well-known psychoanalyst and author) began analysis with Karl Abraham, Freud wrote him a letter advising that Deutsch's marriage not be—in biographer Paul Roazen's words—"disrupted by analysis." In fact, Deutsch's analysis did disrupt her marriage, physically as well as emotionally. She moved to Berlin in order to see Dr. Abraham, leaving her husband behind in Vienna, and while she did not fall in love with Abraham, clearly her analysis pushed her marriage aside for a significant period.

Deutsch's earlier analysis with Freud himself was even more compelling—and tinged with sexuality. Roazen reports that for a time during this analysis Deutsch believed Freud to be in love with her. Moreover, "toward Freud himself," Roazen writes, "Helene had feelings of religious awe. He remained a godlike figure to her for the rest of her life"—a situation that was far from flattering to Deutsch's husband. Of course, according to Roazen, Felix Deutsch was never in the running for godlike stature in his wife's estimation, Freud or no Freud, and, in fact, their relationship after analysis seems to have been much as it was before. Still, as Freud saw, the possibility of disruption was clearly present, and it did occur.

Just how far disruption can go when individual therapy mixes in with a relationship is apparent in the case of Bill and Laura. Their problems began when Laura, having gone into a deep depression, began seeing a male therapist six hours a week. Bill resented this situation immensely, partly because of the money her therapy was costing and partly because he felt Laura was confiding in her therapist instead of in him. Soon her therapy became a major issue between them.

It had to. Subtly, Laura's therapist was taking her side, issuing various "warnings" against Bill. At one point, for example, Bill agreed to come with Laura for joint sessions—but only if their joint session took the place of one of Laura's private sessions. Laura was seeing her therapist three times a week, two hours each session, and Bill was not willing to add a fourth two-hour session to the tab. Laura was not working at the time—another source of contention—and although she was collecting unemployment, Bill was supporting her for the most part.

When Laura presented this scheme to her therapist he made a prediction. Bill, he said, would come with her to therapy for a few sessions and then quit, and when he quit he would not go back to paying for this third session for Laura alone. What was more, he added, Bill was not going to like him.

Every aspect of this forecast proved true. Bill did not like Laura's therapist, attended only a handful of sessions, and when he quit he refused to pay for her third session. Laura's therapist was right, but when a relationship is in trouble, being right is not the only thing you pay a therapist for. By making these predictions, Laura's therapist set himself up as Bill's adversary before Bill ever set foot in his office. He further positioned

Bill as a threat to Laura's therapy. Actions like these caused Laura to see her therapist as, in her word, "protective" of her. While it is great to have a protector— and Laura continues to appreciate her therapist's protectiveness—when what you are being protected from is your *mate*, that is a problem. Essentially, Laura's therapist was teaming up with Laura against Bill.

Soon Bill began seeing his own therapist, a woman. Some sessions into his private therapy, he asked Laura to come with him. She did. By now communication between the two of them had broken down so completely that the only time they were really talking was during the sessions with Bill's therapist. One day Bill came home from a private session and announced that Laura would not be coming with him anymore. She was stunned and she pressed to know whether his therapist agreed with this move. Bill said it was his decision, but that his therapist had agreed to it.

Furious, Laura waited until Bill had left for his session and then called his therapist. She said she was angry that this decision had been made without her, and added that her relationship with Bill would not survive this last blow to what little connection was left between them. Bill's therapist replied, "I have to tell you, Bill's welfare comes first with me." When Laura protested, the therapist said she could not talk, a patient was waiting. That patient was Bill, and Laura knew it. Laura said she needed to talk; the therapist agreed that they would and then hung up. She never called Laura back.

Soon after this Laura moved into her own place. Today neither she nor Bill knows exactly why their relationship came to an end, and neither feels altogether convinced that the relationship *should* have ended. While only they can sort these issues out, it seems clear that their respective therapists worked against their relationship.

A marriage counselor has told me that she can count on one hand the number of marriages she has seen end without a third party involved. While the third party may not create a couple's problems in the first place, he or she certainly plays a crucial role in pushing those problems over the line. This is what happened to Laura and Bill. They had serious problems going into therapy, which individual therapy made worse. Willingly or not, their therapists became the interlopers when Laura and Bill stopped trusting each other and started trusting only their therapists, talking to their therapists instead of to each other.

Worse yet, both therapists put their patients' needs first—above the needs of the relationship. This is dangerous because a relationship is not just two people sharing quarters; it is essentially a third entity that needs as much care and attention as do the individuals involved, particularly when it is in trouble. Shining the spotlight entirely on the individual can blur the relationship into shadow.

Also, too exclusive a focus on the individual can exaggerate his complaints while rendering the relationship's strengths all but invisible. As many patients have remarked, devoting session after session to problems you are having with family, friends, and lovers tends to make your troubles with those loved ones seem *worse.* Yet therapy is by definition concerned with a patient's problems. For a patient to spend an hour talking about what a great weekend she had with a lover would register—to her and to her therapist—as a waste of therapy time and money.

What is more, therapy is by nature concerned with the intricate detail and nuance of social interaction. In therapy you examine every aspect of your painful feel-

ings, reporting every facet of your lover's latest trans-
gression—tone, manner, word choice, and all the rest.
Therapy excels at this sort of intricate investigation, of
course, but it has its drawbacks. You can easily get into
a can't-see-the-forest-for-the-trees dilemma. Or, as one
man who was involved in a new and frequently stormy
relationship put it, "We would have a great Monday,
then a terrible Tuesday, and in her therapy Monday
would disappear. My question was always, 'What happened to Monday?'"

It is up to the therapist to counter this built-in tendency toward the negative by actively intervening in
his patient's stream of association. He must ask his patient to consider what is right with his relationships as
well as what is wrong. If your therapist does not do
this, your therapy may be hurting more than it is helping.

Of course, it is not a simple matter for a therapist to
change course in this manner. A sensitive therapist
takes his cues from his patients, and when you continually come to therapy furious with your lover or
spouse, your therapist is justified in concluding that
what you want is his help in getting out of the relationship—which may or may not be the case. Ellen, a
woman who was painfully in love with a married man,
frequently sought her therapist's aid and support in
breaking off the relationship. Each breakup would last
several days, then the two would reconcile. Meanwhile,
her therapist was in a no-win situation. Concerned for
her patient, she could hardly encourage a relationship
with a married man. But by supporting Ellen's desire
to end it, she was inevitably working against what was,
in fact, a potentially viable relationship.

Moreover, the patient, not the therapist, sets the
goals of his therapy. Ellen's goals were unclear. While
the best of all possible worlds would have been a happy

marriage of her own with her already married lover, that did not seem to be an option. As a result, Ellen was torn between wanting to stay in the relationship and wanting to go. In response, Ellen's therapist spent a great deal of time trying to help her figure out which it was going to be. And, of course, trying to decide whether to stay with a relationship is quite different from trying to understand how to make it better. Not surprisingly, Ellen soon began to feel a real tension between her therapy and her relationship—a tension she finally resolved by leaving therapy. Once out of therapy, she discovered, she and her lover grew closer because they were now tackling together the problems Ellen had been taking outside their relationship, to her therapist. Two years later, Ellen and her lover married.

While it is wonderful to have a smart, caring professional *on your side always,* in some cases it may not be an entirely good thing. The decision to stay with your therapist or leave must be based on your progress— both inside and outside therapy.

If, for example, you are in love with your therapist, you should take a close look at what is going on inside your therapy. Is your therapist subtly encouraging your feelings? Do you have an attraction to unattainable objects that therapy is doing little to change? Has therapy become part of the problem? You might want to talk the situation over with friends, family, or another therapist who is not connected with your current therapist. Time is a key element: if you've been in love with your therapist for years, this is not good therapy. Period. The best that can be said of this situation is that your therapy is not progressing; the worst is that your therapy is making a real relationship impossible. You should find a new therapist, or leave therapy altogether. But if it has been only a few months you may simply be in the throes of an intense—and intensely productive—transference. You can afford to wait and see.

Unfortunately, you can find yourself facing thornier problems than falling in love with a therapist. Romantic love has the virtue at least of being a clear-cut state: you know what you are feeling. While it is hard to leave a therapist you are head over heels in love with, it is not so hard to figure out that perhaps you *should* leave. It is the subtler forms of attachment that make any decision difficult. Most patients become very attached to their therapists, so how do you know if you are too attached?

Basically, you are too attached when therapy is working against your love life rather than for it. Unfortunately, this is not an easy judgment to make. Much of it hinges on whether your therapist is encouraging an overattachment. In thinking over your therapy, the following guidelines should help.

Most obviously, a good therapist does not behave seductively. And there are all kinds of seductions beyond the purely sexual; think of the Hollywood therapist who was diagnosing genius in his patients. A therapist who constantly offers praise and overt reassurance risks setting himself up as the one and only person who is truly behind you, the one and only person you truly need. A good therapist does not encourage this sort of dependency. Instead, he forces you to rely on friends and loved ones for reassurance, keeping them safely ensconced in your affection and need. The therapist's job is not to deliver the best pep talks of anyone you know, but to help you approach the point at which you can deliver your own.

A good therapist will also always try to orient you in the real world, away from the potentially insular world of the fifty-minute hour. Therapy can be incredibly absorbing; in the thick of it you might think of little else. I once met a man who, during initial business meetings with new clients, invariably told the entire tale of his therapy, which, amazingly enough, he had terminated some time before. Obviously he was a man too wrapped up in therapy. A therapist can act to encourage this kind of obsessive focus or to point you back out to the world and the people in it.

An overly heavy-handed insistence on a transference analysis can also foster an obsession with therapy. Gordon, a patient who had begun to see a psychiatrist when he was in the throes of deciding between his wife and his lover, was nonplussed by his doctor's constant investigation of his transference. "I would describe a dream," Gordon says, "in which my wife and my lover were both in a classroom together while I was standing outside, and he would say my dream was actually about therapy." To his growing dismay, Gordon found that his psychiatrist interpreted each and every dream he brought in as being yet another dream about therapy.

Not surprisingly, at least two of this doctor's women patients were completely in love with him—too much so. One of them had centered her life around her therapy sessions with him for many years; the other had just started therapy and was showing every sign of becoming equally enthralled. It is unlikely that this was sheer coincidence; an analyst who constantly positions himself at the center of his patients' unconscious dreams will probably convince at least a few of them that he is the object most worthy of their conscious dreams as well.

How does a therapist avoid becoming the center of your attention? In large part by encouraging communication with other people in your life. Marilyn's therapy offers an excellent example of this strategy. Marilyn had just begun to see a male therapist when she met Joe, the man she would eventually marry. Because she and Joe encountered a number of troubles in their early days, Marilyn frequently arrived at therapy bearing a fresh tale of woe concerning their relationship. Invariably, when this happened, her therapist's first response was to ask whether she had talked to Joe about it.

The effect of this standing query was to steer her back toward Joe. The truth was, she always discussed problems with Joe—keeping things to herself wasn't the difficulty. Her therapist probably knew this, but by continuing to ask whether she had talked to Joe, he repeatedly signaled that Joe was an important person to talk to—as important as a therapist.

Fortunately, Joe was also seeing a therapist who gave him the same signals. Once, at the end of a session in which Joe had talked out an argument he was having with Marilyn, his therapist said, "So what Marilyn has been saying makes a lot of sense." Since Joe had already arrived at the same conclusion that Marilyn was probably right, he did not feel his therapist was taking sides against him. Very diplomatically Joe's therapist had made Joe feel that in his view Marilyn's opinions and feelings were important and, in certain cases, right. Both therapists were working *for* their clients' relationship by asking the two to focus on what the other felt and meant. Neither sought to become the *authority;* neither angled to win for himself a position as most trusted person.

Moreover, both therapists encouraged Marilyn and Joe to consider their own roles in the problems they were having. Once, when what should have been a mere spat had escalated into a two-week standoff, Marilyn's therapist stepped in to save the day. The quarrel had begun one Sunday morning when Marilyn had said something sharp about Joe and his ex-wife. Joe did not respond right away, though he was obviously annoyed.

Some moments later, when the conversation shifted to a job interview Marilyn had gone on earlier in the week, Joe volunteered the opinion that Marilyn had blown it; she had probably been too aggressive, he now said.

Marilyn was angry and hurt. She badly wanted the job, and Joe had been cheering her on all week. Now it was clear to her that he was withdrawing support because he was angry over her remark about his ex-wife. But when she said as much to Joe, he adamantly denied that the one had anything to do with the other. He wasn't angry, he said, he was just trying to tell her she'd been overly assertive. He was trying to *help*.

Joe's denial made Marilyn furious, mainly because she saw it as emblematic of how their relationship was going, and how it would continue to go in the future. "I could see this whole scenario stretching out before me," she says, "where Joe was always going to be the good guy and I was always going to be the villain; Joe was never going to admit to being in the wrong. He had really hurt me, and instead of apologizing, he blamed *me* for overanalyzing things."

Marilyn was mad and, as Joe steadfastly denied any but the most benign of motives, she stayed mad; neither Joe nor she would budge. Finally Marilyn's therapist, after hearing about the standoff for two full weeks, bent his rules and gave Marilyn a piece of direct advice. (And that is another aspect of a good therapist: flexibility, a capacity to improvise.) Analyzing the situation was getting them nowhere, so Marilyn's therapist allowed himself to shift into the "Dear Abby" mode for one crucial moment. Very gently he said, "When you talk to Joe tonight, try not to attack him, because when you get someone's back up against the wall, he has to defend himself." While this piece of wisdom was pure common sense, it came as a revelation to Marilyn. Suddenly she saw clearly that although she was right on substance, she was wrong on approach; she was leaving Joe no room to admit error.

Marilyn met Joe for dinner after therapy. For some minutes the two of them sat in tense dialogue over wine and bread. Although Marilyn was trying to be less hostile, Joe wasn't coming around. Finally Marilyn simply said, "Why can't you just admit that I said something mean to you, so you said something mean to me?" Joe looked at her, obviously surprised. "Is that all?" he said.

This was certainly a charge he had no problem pleading guilty to—especially since it included an admission of guilt on Marilyn's side as well—and he did so, at once. All Marilyn had wanted was some acknowledgment from Joe of his part in the dispute, and she felt better immediately.

After that they were able to talk about what had been going on. From Joe's point of view, Marilyn had been so angry that he assumed she was accusing him of committing a monstrous deed—which he hadn't, and which he certainly refused to confess to. From Marilyn's point of view, Joe was incapable of admitting any wrongdoing whatsoever. Both were seeing the argument writ large. In this case, Marilyn's therapist helped put things in perspective.

Joe's therapist also responded helpfully. In therapy, Joe was able to see that he did indeed—as Marilyn believed—have difficulty admitting he was wrong. Furthermore, he tended to disown all feelings of anger: it was very hard for him to admit that he could feel angry at a woman he loved, or that he could say something hurtful out of anger. In truth, he *did* want to be seen as the good guy in his relationships, and he was quite capable of making covertly hostile remarks in order to keep his image unsullied. His therapist helped him see that this way of expressing anger had taken a serious toll on his former marriage and was now working some real damage on his relationship with Marilyn as well. While Marilyn was probably overreacting, she was not wrong. This was a powerful moment for Joe, a moment in which he began to change his way of relating to women.

Both therapists in this situation helped Marilyn and Joe to look at what each was doing wrong; neither therapist took sides, though both made their patients feel fully supported. As a result, Marilyn and Joe's relationship took several giant steps forward. When a few months later Marilyn arrived for therapy with the announcement that she and Joe had become engaged, her therapist broke into a broad smile and offered his congratulations. He deserved to be happy; he had made a real contribution to the new marriage that was to be.

When you look at a situation like Marilyn and Joe's you see what therapy is like when it is working *for* its patients' love lives. And this is the standard by which your therapy must be judged. Even if you have no romantic problems to speak of, you should still make sure that your therapist has not come to loom larger in your life than the people you love. Because sorting out the multitude of causes that go into creating unhappiness in love is probably impossible (especially when it is your own life you are trying to analyze), the question to ask yourself is not whether therapy is interfering with your love life, but whether it is actively *helping* your love life. If not, it may be time to find a new therapist. Or to leave altogether.

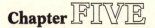

TIES THAT BIND: CONFIDING IN YOUR THERAPIST

People tell secrets to their therapists that they may never have told another soul. In return, their therapists promise absolute discretion. And that is the basis of the therapeutic contract: you agree to tell your secrets because your therapist agrees to keep them.

Therapy could not proceed without this agreement, but therapeutic secrecy has its down side. Too much secrecy can bind you too closely to your therapist, distancing you from friends and family. Secrecy divides people into insiders and outsiders, and when your friends and lovers become the outsiders, you run the danger of getting mired in therapy.

Judith's experience bears this out. In her early thirties Judith suffered a number of setbacks in her work. With a partner, she had opened a company that failed; she took a job and soon after was fired. It was too much, and she became profoundly depressed. When she found another job she began using cocaine to get through the days.

She kept her cocaine use to herself, not even telling Dan, the man with whom she had lived for several years. She told only her new therapist, sharing solely with him not only a secret of major proportions but one that powerfully affected her life with Dan.

Dan seems to have sensed Judith's secrecy. He soon began to complain that she was shutting him out, that she was talking to her therapist but not to him. For her part, Judith felt that, in fact, Dan didn't *want* her to talk to him unless she was going to tell him what he wanted to hear. It seemed to her that Dan wasn't interested in bad news, and at this point Judith was in such a slump that bad news was all she had to share. Her therapist was the only person she had now who would listen to all the pain.

Whatever the truth of the matter—and probably it was a case of both partners being right to some degree—their relationship did not survive. By the time Judith finally did reveal her drug problem to Dan, long after she had stopped using cocaine, he no longer cared as he once had. He wanted out. Soon after, they separated.

Tellingly, Judith and her therapist have continued together to this day. Judith is strongly attached to him; he is probably the person with whom she is most intimate. He knows more about her than anyone else does.

But did Judith's turning to her therapist amount to a turning away from Dan? While she did not think so, certainly Dan experienced her therapy that way, and perhaps this is what matters in making such a judgment. In any case, a clear principle emerges from Judith and Dan's experience: if your partner feels that you and your therapist are shutting him out, you should take the matter seriously.

It is easy enough to see why a lover or spouse might feel excluded by therapy. Intimacy between men and women (or between friends or relatives) is based on sharing. Lovers and spouses share their bodies, their homes, their thoughts, their worldly goods. What is more, between mates there is usually a presumption of exclusive sharing—of monogamous commitment. Monogamy does not end with sex. There is a monogamy of information, too; most couples recognize certain subjects or experiences that are private to them as a couple. Only they know these things about themselves and their life together.

This sort of "couples privacy" is important; it helps a couple feel like a couple. Secrets work the same way; in fact, often they are simply a more adamant form of privacy. They bond the secret-keepers together, and separate them from those not "in the know." You can see this function of secrecy at its most elemental among children. In the shifting alliances of childhood, secrets play a crucial role. When a trio of friends splinters off into two friends and one outcast, for example, secrets always figure in. Suddenly the new duo knows a secret the left-out third does not.

Adults may wield secrecy more subtly, but the princi ple remains the same. Those "in the know" occupy the inner circle, over and apart from those "in the dark." Tell someone a secret about yourself, and inevitably you feel closer to that person, as he or she does to you. Quite understandably, then, when one member of a couple starts telling all to an outside party, the other member may have mixed feelings. Some partners may feel betrayed because their confidences are not being kept. Others may feel left out. Still others may feel defensive, worried that the secrets being kept between therapist and patient are secrets *about them*.

As with Judith and Dan, once one partner starts keeping secrets with his or her therapist, things can go from bad to worse. If you belong to a couple, it is important not to set up a situation in which your therapist is hearing truths you don't tell your mate. Such truths are apt to be painful, and if you dump all the "bad stuff" on your therapist while keeping up a good front for your mate or lover, you will inevitably come to feel that only your therapist really understands or cares for you as you are. Most people do not have psychic room for more than one dearest friend or mate. If your therapist slides into this position, others may slip out.

Of course, telling your mate all poses its own hazards. Taking the most extreme case, suppose you are having an affair, which you discuss in therapy. Do you tell your mate? In deciding, the point to remember is that if you are having affairs continuously, which you discuss only with your therapist, you are probably not having much of a relationship with your mate. Your sexual intimacy is with your other lovers; your emotional intimacy is with your therapist; not much is left over for your mate.

Assuming that you want to save your relationship, something has to change. The affairs have to end, or the exclusive soul-searching with the therapist has to end, or both—preferably both. In this situation you and your mate should head for joint therapy with a couples counselor: at least that way you will be doing something of significance *together*.

Patients often hide what is going on in therapy simply to spare their mates' feelings. Should you tell your mate that in today's session you complained nonstop about him or her? The answer is a clear yes and no. First off, it is essential *not* to set your therapist up as your "second." Laura and Bill provide the cautionary tale here: nothing drives a mate away so fast as the feeling that you are telling on him or her at your therapist's office. In line with this, never use your therapist to say things you don't want to say yourself. "My therapist thinks you're insensitive to my feelings" clearly means "I think you're insensitive to my feelings," only it's twice as irritating. When you hide behind your therapist this way you allow your mate no response: after all, your therapist is the expert.

Reporting back from therapy is a delicate matter. You need to reveal enough to feel as connected to your mate as you do to your therapist—without alienating your mate in the process. The most diplomatic approach is to briefly summarize a session in the "mea culpa" terms a good therapist helps you come to, reporting honestly what therapy is showing you about your own contribution to your problems.

This summary should *not* take the form of a roundabout accusation, such as "I know I've been withdrawn lately, and in thinking it over I realize it's probably because you've been so involved in your work. I'm probably withdrawing as a defense, because unconsciously I feel as if I can't count on you." This kind of mea culpa is no mea culpa at all; it is an updated, therapeutic finger-pointing that preempts the accused's opportunity for defense. The only thing being said here, ostensibly, is that the speaker *unconsciously* feels the other can't be counted upon. The real message ("you are unreliable") is being turned into a sensitive expression of therapeutic insight ("my unconscious thinks you are unreliable"). Of course, no one can argue with somebody else's unconscious.

Keeping a mate posted on your therapy is considerably easier when your therapy session has been more about you than about him or her. In this case couples often summarize each session to their mates the day it takes place. A one-sentence formulation can suffice: "I was talking to my therapist today about how I always seem to procrastinate more when the stakes are higher." Sometimes these encapsulations lead to fuller discussion and sometimes they don't. Nothing is forced, and that is the crucial point. Both partners should feel that the issue or problem is an open subject between them; it is not just happening between one partner and his or her therapist.

This feeling of openness is usually all you need to head off the potential competition between mate and therapist. When they are not made to feel shut out, most people are happy to have a loved one in therapy. After all, your friends and family want happiness for you, and if they feel your therapist is an ally in achieving that end, they are all for his or her presence in your life.

If you are not part of a couple, it may be even more important not to rely exclusively on your therapist as father (or mother) confessor. Single people often fan out among a number of friends, so that they may see any particular friend only once every few weeks or so. If you live alone, your therapist can easily become the one person you confide in most often. And when you feel that your therapist is the only person truly close to you, you can get stuck. Try to stay close to friends. Tell them what's bothering you, enough so that you feel they know you well and care. Communication with friends, family, and lovers—about yourself *and* about your therapy—can keep your therapy moving.

Of course, apart from the secrets you may be keeping from others, therapeutic secrecy also involves the "secrets" your therapist keeps from you. Following psychoanalytic theory, therapists keep their lives and thoughts to themselves in order to help the patient. They strive to become largely neutral figures, "blank screens" onto which their patients can easily project past figures from their lives. Therapists also avoid talking about themselves in order to "make room" for the patient. Most people arrive at therapy in a state of pain and confusion; they don't understand why their lives seem to be going so badly. A therapist—and there are some—who talks about himself each session, who gives Dear Abby–like advice to his patients, can easily become the "fearless leader," the dominant personality in the room. When this happens, the patient fades. Therapists who decline to talk about themselves or to offer direct advice and opinions allow the patient—shaky as he may be—to become the most visible person present.

On the one hand the therapist's self-concealment is a sensitive and effective approach to treating patients who come to therapy at a point of real vulnerability, but on the other, this approach can sometimes work against the patient's interests. Consider the case of Susan. A lesbian herself, Susan was seeing a woman therapist who she had good reason to believe was also gay (mutual friends within the gay community had confirmed this). One of Susan's main problems was a long history of powerful fantasy attachments to unattainable objects, and, predictably, she soon found herself overwhelmed by secret longing and desire for her therapist. She felt strongly that her therapist's insistence on revealing nothing whatsoever of herself in therapy encouraged her fantasies. She did not know whether, in fact, her therapist was gay or if she was seriously involved with someone. If Susan had known these basics, she believed, her therapist would have seemed more "real" to her; instead she found herself creating a woman who would respond to her love.

Finally, overwhelmed by the fantasies she was nurturing, Susan wrote her therapist a letter in which she said, "I need some facts about you so I can have some grounding in reality." One week after the letter had been sent, Susan's father died. The very next day, in desperate need of comfort, Susan went to therapy. It was in this session that her therapist chose to respond to the letter (odd in itself since she had ignored pre-

vious letters from Susan) by saying—and this is a direct quotation—"Here are the rules." The rules, she
stated, were that their relationship was to be strictly
professional in nature, that when therapy was over
they would have no further contact. They would not be
friends; certainly, she made clear, they would not be
lovers.

For Susan this was devastating. She had just suffered
the profound loss of her father; now her therapist, with
whom she was in love, whom she fantasized continuing
a rich friendship with after therapy, was rejecting her.
The timing was cruel. Reeling from her father's death,
Susan experienced these "rules" as both a rejection *and*
a rebuke. She must have done something terribly
wrong, she felt, to have provoked this scene. She spent
the remaining months of her therapy trying to "make
things all better" because she felt responsible for what
had happened; she felt like a failure.

Very probably Susan's therapy would have been
more effective if her therapist had given her some information about her private life—real information, as
opposed to "rules." Freud himself was flexible on this
point. Although he counseled neutrality, in fact he
practiced out of his home, where patients were sometimes introduced to his family. Having witnessed first-
hand their analyst's private identity as family man, if
Freud's patients fell in love with him, they did so
knowing that their fantasy was just that, a fantasy.

Furthermore, if Susan had not felt that her therapist
was keeping secrets from her, her therapy would not
have left her feeling so small and vulnerable. In the
social world at large secrecy always separates the
"higher" from the "lower." Parents keep secrets from
children; doctors keep secrets from patients; national
leaders keep secrets from the public. Studies bear out
the fact that at a personal level one-sided self-revela-

tion—precisely what takes place in therapy—increases the authority of the listener, while decreasing the status of the speaker.

In Susan's case, she was essentially being *infantilized* by her therapy. Her therapist's insensitivity after her father's death provoked in her the classic reaction of a hurt child. Instead of challenging her therapist's judgment, Susan responded meekly. She felt somehow to blame for what had happened, and when she wasn't blaming herself she was inventing excuses for her therapist's behavior. Her therapist confirmed Susan's childlike position when she chose the word "rules" to characterize her professional policy against becoming intimate with patients. Small and hurt, Susan felt bad for having broken the rules. And her therapist's insistence upon absolute secrecy when it came to her own private life freeze-locked Susan in this diminished role.

Therapeutic secrecy poses another problem for some patients: it exerts a strong gravitational pull and can make leaving therapy difficult. You stall simply because you cannot leave until you know how the story "ends." Therapeutic secrecy is particularly gripping because not only does the therapist know secrets about himself and secrets about you, he also knows *secrets you are keeping from yourself*. The fundamental premise of Freudian psychology is that people know things they don't know they know. This is the function of the unconscious: to repress information you wish to avoid. But even when it is repressed, it is still there, within you. You know it but you don't know it.

Your therapist, on the other hand, *does* know it. Of course, your therapist is not able to divine that long-forgotten afternoon in late 1960 when you stole five dollars from your mother's purse; he senses secret feelings, not secret facts. A large part of a therapist's job is to discern what is going on inside patients, then to help them make these discoveries for themselves. And this process is entirely indirect; a therapist never simply tells you what he knows—or suspects—to be true of you.

The fact that your therapist in effect knows and keeps secrets about you can prolong therapy indefinitely. You can't leave, because you *want to know* what he knows. You went into therapy in the first place because you wanted to know; now, months or even years down the line, you still want to know. Therapeutic secrecy makes closure, a true *end* to therapy, very difficult.

Many therapists are sensitive to the issues raised by therapeutic secrecy, and many handle it by trying to adopt a reassuring flexibility: they do not usually volunteer personal or professional information, but they do not withhold it altogether when asked.

Jack's therapist provides a good example of handling a patient's request for professional information with real tact. Jack had been seeing his therapist for two years when his insurance coverage changed, and the new policy required a statement from Jack's therapist diagnosing his condition. Since Jack had never received a "diagnosis" from him, this was a moment of truth. His therapist filled out the form and returned it to Jack, who discovered for the first time that, in his therapist's view, he was suffering from a "depressive disorder with narcissistic features."

This characterization took him aback. He hadn't thought of himself as depressed. He had thought of himself as narcissistic pure and simple. Since his entire generation had been accused of narcissism, he supposed he was no different; "narcissism" as a diagnosis was something he could live with. But "depressive disorder" sounded weak to him, and sad. Not that he would have *liked* seeing a black-and-white confirmation of his supposed narcissism, but he found the term "depressive disorder" both depressing and daunting.

At his next session he asked his therapist what exactly he meant by the designation "depressive disorder with narcissistic features." His therapist answered that in fact he had never formulated an official diagnosis of Jack, that he had done so now only for the purposes of the insurance form. He had used "depressive disorder," he went on to say, because Jack had been depressed over his divorce when he first came to therapy.

This was a tactful—and circumspect—answer. Notice that Jack's therapist left as much unsaid as said —he made no mention of the meaning of "narcissistic features," for instance. But, on the other hand, he offered a truthful and plausible account of the phrase "depressive disorder." And by saying that he had not so labeled Jack from the beginning, he made clear he did not see Jack as simply a case—yet another depressive-disorder-with-narcissistic-features in a long career of treating depressive-disorders-with-narcissistic-features. Most important, he gave Jack the feeling that he would willingly answer questions. He did not, by either tone or suggestion, cut off the exchange.

A flexible therapist fields questions from patients by giving enough information to satisfy, but not enough to distress. By and large, such therapists usually do not volunteer information, but will tell you what you need to know, when you need to know it. In short, Freud's original impulse to make the therapist as neutral as possible—*without* becoming unreal—was right. If your therapist shows a lack of flexibility, you may want to consider whether it is interfering with your therapy's progress toward a sound and healthy conclusion.

MIND OVER MONEY

Down to brass tacks. Therapists practice therapy for a living. Especially for therapists in private practice, each patient adds directly to gross income—a figure that may not be as high as patients commonly assume. Within the profession, a full load is considered to be twenty to twenty-five contact hours per week. For a clinical psychologist working the standard week at an average of $80 an hour, this amounts to a gross of $1,600 to $2,000 a week, or $80,000 to $100,000 a year. Of course, many therapists earn much less, and a therapist in private practice has no institutional backing: no benefits, no unemployment insurance, no pension. He must also pay his own overhead, and office rentals in major urban areas run as high as $1,500 a month. All of which means that when a patient wants to leave therapy, any money worries the therapist may have are apt to come rushing to the fore. For the therapist, your termination is not only about your getting well. It is about finding a new patient to take your place.

And new patients are not always that easy to come by—especially given the relatively low insurance benefits available for psychotherapy. Typically, insurance covers only 50 percent of the cost of a psychotherapy session, compared to 80 percent of the cost of an office visit to a physician. Because patients must carry more and more of the financial burden for therapy themselves, some people who would have gone into therapy if their insurance covered it are now choosing to forgo it.

As a result, competition for new patients is increasing. Under these circumstances, facing the prospect of drumming up new business can be disturbing indeed. Much better for the therapist's peace of mind—and for the security of family members who depend on him or her—to see patients who are in therapy for the long haul. And small wonder that the profession has produced an entire literature advocating high fees as a means of securing the patient's commitment to therapy.

As a group, therapists are ambivalent about the issue of fees. One survey found that 60 percent of therapists "experienced inner conflict" over the setting of fees. This conflict ranged from guilt over taking money from needy people to resentment of the way some patients manipulated them into accepting lower fees than they could actually afford. Therapists who had moved up in social class often felt guilty over doing better than their parents. Others adamantly set very high fees and maintained them even when seeing patients who were not well-off.

Scan the literature of the profession and you discern a very real discomfort with the subject of money. Freud saw money as symbolic excrement, which means that a patient angling to save money on fees becomes more than a little suspect in the world according to Freud (as does the therapist who is openly preoccupied with *making* money on fees). Among Freud's descendants, statements like the following, from a psychoanalyst, are not uncommon: "All of the bargain hunters whom I have observed clinically have been orally regressed neurotics." Here we have moved from the anal to the oral, but the critical stance is just as apparent. Repeatedly in the writings of psychoanalysis you find a strongly negative attitude toward money and those who hope to amass it.

In short, therapists themselves are not entirely comfortable with the subject of money in general, or fees in particular. This attitude might account for the emphasis the profession places on the psychological importance of fees, not to the therapist, but to the *patient*. Many psychologists, psychiatrists, and analysts believe that the amount of money a patient pays for his therapy is directly related to the amount of effort he puts into it. A patient is thought to get what he pays for: if he pays a lot relative to his income, he gets a lot, because he puts in a lot. The more you pay, the greater your commitment to seeing your therapy through. Ergo, high fees are good for the patient.

The corollary to the fee-equals-commitment equation is the practice many therapists maintain of charging for missed sessions. The logic behind this is that because therapy is painful, patients would prefer to dodge sessions. Allowing patients to cancel without penalty is tantamount to rewarding them for irresponsible behavior toward therapy.

Patients almost invariably object to this practice strenuously. Mike's story is a classic example. For two years Mike had seen his therapist without missing a session. Then one day, several hours before he was scheduled to appear in his therapist's office, he twisted his ankle so badly while running that he could not walk. A friend drove him to the hospital, where, in the midst of signing forms and contending with emergency room nurses, he nevertheless managed to hobble to a pay phone to let his psychiatrist know he would be missing that day's appointment.

His psychiatrist charged him for the session anyway. Mike was furious. "And the worst part of it," he says, "was having to pay not only for a session I never had but for the next session, which we spent arguing about the bill. We didn't talk about either my divorce or my career, but about *his* billing policy. For the entire hour. And I paid for it." As many patients have learned the hard way, that is the rub when arguing with therapists about their fees: you pay for the argument, literally.

Agreeing to come for more than one session a week is also often seen as a sign of serious commitment to therapy—a form of commitment that also guarantees higher earnings for the therapist. Megan, a free-lance writer earning $18,000 a year, was constantly exhorted by her analyst to see him more frequently. She attended sessions once a week, and in every session her doctor urged her to commit to two, three, or even four weekly visits. Megan found this surprising, considering her modest and erratic income. As a free-lancer she did not know when the next check was due; months could pass without any income at all. Naturally, months could not pass without paying for therapy. Megan was absolutely on her own financially; she had no fallback position if her bills got out of hand. The price her doctor was charging, $75 a week, was absolutely the most she could afford to spend on her therapy.

And yet, when she pleaded relative poverty as her reason for not increasing her number of sessions, her analyst dismissed this claim as specious. In his view the reason she would not come twice a week was resistance. Megan did not want to *commit* to therapy, he said.

Could this be true? Certainly Megan did not think so, and research suggests she is right. A classic study by Kenneth Pope, Jesse Geller, and Leland Wilkinson found that patients who paid nothing at all for their therapy improved at the same rate as patients who paid the entire fee out of pocket. Furthermore, patients who paid nothing were just as reliable about showing up for sessions as patients who paid in full, and they remained in therapy for the same number of sessions overall.

In actual practice, most therapists behave as if they agree with these findings. You never hear of a therapist insisting that a patient with full coverage pay for therapy himself in order to ensure his commitment. Nor do you see therapists turning away young adults whose parents are footing the bill. And, of course, therapists do not see their own level of commitment as being adversely affected by low fees. No professional would put in more or less effort depending on the fee—and few if any professionals would argue that *unconsciously* a therapist shirks his responsibilities when accepting a lower fee.

In short, the psychological theory of fees rests on the assumption that what is good for the therapist is also good for the patient: in the linking of money and commitment the therapist's need to earn money is translated into the patient's need to spend money. This linkage may serve as an important defense for the therapist. Good therapy can be painful at times, and the good therapist often has to be willing to risk alienating —even losing—his patient in order to help. When a therapist frankly confronts the fact that he needs his patients financially, he may be less willing to take that chance. For sound professional reasons, no therapist wants to feel financially vulnerable to his patients.

Of course, the therapist's vulnerability is substantially reduced when patients sign on for long-term therapy. Again, the widespread belief among therapists that long-term therapy is superior to short-term may be influenced by psychological factors. The reasoning is that more therapy over more time is better than less therapy over less time because change comes hard and slow. Although a "brief therapy" movement is afoot (brief therapy is a form of treatment in which patients see doctors for periods ranging from a few weeks to a few months only), many therapists view this development with suspicion. As they see it, patients who seek brief therapy are looking for a quick fix; they don't want to do the hard work of real change.

Bernie Zilbergeld spells out the benefits for the therapist of long-term therapy in his *Shrinking of America.* As a practitioner of short-term therapy he needs two new referrals a week in order to keep his practice full. A therapist friend of his who practices long-term therapy needs only four referrals a *year* in order to maintain her practice, which is twice as large as his.

Certainly therapists do not deliberately forge psychiatric theory to fit their financial needs—far from it. Therapists know therapy works, and when you know that what you are doing is effective, you are likely to think that doing more of it is better than doing less. Moreover, therapists possess an unconscious just like everyone else. A new therapist enters his profession *financially* needing long-term patients while *philosophically* having been taught the superiority of long-term therapy, and the two dovetail nicely. A theory that says high fees and long-term therapy and multiple sessions a week and charges for missed sessions are good for patients is appealing because it allays a therapist's concerns on every front.

• • •

Money conflicts abound on the patient's side as well. Many, many patients take advantage of a therapist's sliding scale in order to be assigned a low fee, then neglect to inform their therapist of a recent raise. Since presumably therapy is at least partially responsible for the patient's new success, this is particularly galling to therapists. They feel the fee should rise not only because the patient can now afford to pay it, but also because therapy has helped him achieve this happy state of affairs.

Many patients resent their therapist's fees. They see therapy as a kind of financial bloodsucker instead of as a desired service for which they are paying. Some patients actually see themselves as martyred to therapy. One man told his new lover that he wished he could take her out to an expensive restaurant, but could not because he had to pay for therapy. Being in therapy herself, she accepted this state of affairs as entirely reasonable. In fact, it is not. A man who can afford to spend $200 a month on therapy for *years* (as this man had) can certainly scrape together enough spare change to finance one posh evening out. As is often the case, something more than simple finance was involved.

Among patients, his attitude is commonplace. People who are quite willing to spend substantial sums on travel or clothing or houses often become irate, anxious, or resistant when it comes to paying for therapy. Transference is partly responsible. Because of transference you experience your therapist as a combination parent/lover/friend—and parents, lovers, and friends do what they do for free. From a strictly emotional standpoint, when a therapist charges a fee for his services it compromises his position as someone who cares. As one patient put it, "Paying a therapist to listen is a little like paying a prostitute for sex. You put down your money, and she's on your side for the hour. It's an empty experience." In short, quite apart from all rational considerations (your therapist is a trained professional, like any other, whose services you are engaging), at the emotional level paying for therapy can feel slightly demeaning.

Another reason for a patient's tendency to resent fees is that they undermine his need to maintain the therapist as a superior. Therapy is one of the most paradoxical of human relationships: a therapist seems like your higher-up when, in fact, he is your employee. *You* are paying *him*, which means you are theoretically the boss—and yet in therapy the patient is manifestly *not* the boss. Therapy would not work if he were.

Obviously, in most client-professional relationships the client is not the boss the way an employer in business is. When you hire a lawyer or a medical doctor— just as when you hire a therapist—you are recognizing his superior expertise and seeking his counsel. But that is where the similarity ends. When you hire a lawyer you pay him to know more about the law than you do; when you hire a therapist, you hire him, in essence, to know more about *life* than you do. The problem is that while you may have no experience of the law, you have plenty of experience of life. Accordingly, sustaining faith that your therapist is as "superior" to you in knowledge of life as your lawyer is in knowledge of law can be a real challenge. Of course, you may well *want* to "look up" to your therapist, to maintain the illusion that your therapist is all-knowing, and you may strive to do so. Nevertheless, the fact that you are paying your therapist implies that you have some responsibility to evaluate his performance, that you could know better than he whether or not you are getting what you came for.

· · ·

For all of these reasons, therapists are right to "psychologize" their patients' relationship to money. For most patients the fees they pay their therapists *are* highly symbolic. Whatever particular problems the patient is trying to work out in therapy will tend to be reflected in his feelings toward his therapist's fees. Therefore each patient will tend to have a unique attitude and behavior when it comes to paying the bill. Some will pay on time, some will pay late, some will resent fees, some will wish they could afford to pay more, and so on.

Many patients also connect the payment of fees with the position therapy tends to give all patients: that of a child in relation to a parent. In some cases, the structure of therapy encourages this connection. The practice of charging for missed sessions, for example, may make the patient feel like a child who has skipped school. But more often than not, it is the patient who works things so that his payment of fees can be consistent with his feeling of being the child in relation to a grown-up, caring therapist.

For example, patients often go to therapy at their parents' expense, an arrangement that can easily work as a form of not quite leaving the nest. The patient is still tied financially to his parents; symbolically, his parents are paying for someone to take up where they left off. Therapy can be the last stage of growing up. But for this arrangement to be healthy, it has to cease at some point. Either the young patient must take over his own payments, or he should "graduate" from therapy. If he does neither, this initially positive arrangement can turn into a self-perpetuating, negative cycle.

Kevin, now a major Hollywood executive, is a good example of someone who grew up for the second time in therapy. In his late twenties he lacked a sense of direction: he was an adolescent of the '60s and he was smoking a great deal of marijuana, rather lackadaisically trying to become a screenwriter but not really getting much writing done, only sporadically attending the meetings his agent arranged for him. Mainly, he was just hanging out. He had no real forward motion in his life, and he was not happy.

When he went into therapy his mother paid. Furthermore, he went to his mother's therapist. It seems clear that his entering therapy was in part a way of remaining a son. Kevin himself tends to see it this way. Over the next few years his life began to come together. He stopped smoking marijuana, realized he didn't want to be a writer, and found his first job in the film industry. He was operating under his own steam now; he was taking charge. And he left therapy.

"Leaving therapy was definitely part of growing up for me," he says. "I felt like I was an adult, and I could handle my own life." Now in his late thirties, married, and a father, he does not believe he would ever go back into therapy. "If I were to have problems I couldn't handle myself," he says, "I would turn to my wife, or to my friends. I wouldn't want to see a therapist again."

Even if you are paying your therapist's fees yourself, you may still be using therapy to remain symbolically young. Tom and Mary lived through a complicated version of this. In their early thirties, both were in therapy when they met, spending around $200 a month each in fees. Neither was saving money, since their combined salaries amounted to $45,000. While both of them had always seen therapy as a real financial burden, to Mary this burden seemed significantly heavier once she and Tom married. "I had gone into therapy because my love life was a mess," she says, "and now that I was happily married I didn't feel I needed it anymore. But it was more than that—I felt that a grown-up, married woman shouldn't *be* in therapy all the time. I'd been running around like a crazy person all through my twenties; now I wanted to feel as if I had finally arrived, as if I had become an *adult*. I wanted validation of this, but instead my therapist was still treating me as if I were this neurotic girl-woman with a lot of deep-seated problems." Suddenly, therapy was interfering with her self-image as a grown woman whose life was under control. And so, soon after her marriage, she ended treatment.

But Tom, who had been seeing his therapist for a longer period of time, did not share her view. To him, there was no conflict between being married and being in therapy. However, there was the problem of money, particularly in light of the future. For Tom and Mary the future meant children, though they had not quite admitted this to each other—or to themselves. Having been raised in middle-class homes, they also both wanted a house. And on $45,000 in a major city, achieving these goals would be impossible without some sort of savings plan.

Tom and Mary soon discovered that they viewed money very differently. Mary felt that the $200 Tom was spending on therapy every month would be put to better use as savings toward a house. Tom argued, quite reasonably, that at the rate of $200 a month it would take ten years to accumulate the $25,000 necessary for a down payment—and by then they would probably need twice that sum. They could spend the rest of their lives chasing the housing market. While he had always wanted to live in his own home, he simply accepted that he would not be able to.

This line of reasoning, though logical, did not sit well with Mary. Whatever the obstacles to their buying a house, she felt, Tom ought at least to commit himself to the *attempt*. She began to feel that Tom was choosing therapy over their marriage and future offspring. Of course, the fact that she focused her dissatisfaction on therapy is significant to some degree; she could just as easily have decided they were frittering away their potential down payment on their frequent dinners out. But Tom's staying in therapy during the honeymoon period of their new marriage particularly rankled.

The outcome of their story is revealing. After two months of arguing, Tom put his foot down. Mary was not to nag him about leaving therapy anymore. Feeling she was in the wrong, Mary backed off. Then, over the next several months, Tom began to feel that, in fact, this might be a good time to leave therapy. He finally did leave just as he was on the brink of being promoted to a partnership in the architectural firm for which he worked, just as he was "arriving" professionally.

Interestingly, the house issue resolved itself almost immediately. They received notice that their two-bedroom rented house was to be sold; they would have to move, and their rent would double in the process. Tom went immediately to his firm and negotiated a raise somewhat higher than his firm would normally have offered with his promotion, and now that they could afford a mortgage Mary asked her father to loan them the down payment. He agreed, and within a year they were established in their own home. Soon after they conceived their first child.

As with many other stories of leaving therapy, it is impossible to know precisely what led to what. Mary feels strongly that leaving therapy was part of buying the house, that had they both stayed in therapy there might have been no forward movement. To her, leaving therapy was part of moving on, part of leaving their unmarried twenties definitively behind, part of assuming married thirties roles. Tom does not entirely agree, though he, too, is happy with his decision to leave. Of course, leaving therapy does not guarantee you'll get a raise from your firm or a loan from your family, but it *may* put you more in the frame of mind to ask. (And as to families, it may also put your parents more in the frame of mind to agree....)

You could argue that people leave therapy when they get married simply because they have found someone to take their therapist's place, or that they leave therapy when they buy a house because mortgage payments take the place of therapy payments. Both of these arguments are true at one level. But overall, the fact that so many patients leave therapy at major life transitions, like marriage, house-buying, and child-bearing, implies that for them ending therapy is psychologically bound up with leaving youth—no matter what their chronological age at the time.

Unless your therapy is fully covered by insurance, money plays a part in any decision to leave. The problem is that because money is both symbolic and real it is difficult to know if you want to leave therapy because it costs too much or if therapy suddenly costs too much because you want to leave. If you are seeing a therapist who is able to confront the issue of money directly, you can enlist his aid in answering this question. A good therapist will encourage you to spend your money wisely and maturely.

You should always evaluate your therapist's policies concerning fees. The therapist who sets fees on a sliding scale, according to his patients' ability to pay, clearly wants his patients to handle money responsibly, at least when it comes to budgeting for therapy. Moreover, a therapist who sets a sliding scale is acknowledging implicitly that money is real and important *for the patient*. Such a therapist is much less likely to chalk up your money concerns to resistance.

The same principle applies to the missed appointments issue: the therapist who is most likely to support an attitude of financial realism in his patients will tend not to charge for missed appointments when you give sufficient advance notice. But even a therapist who makes none of these concessions may be willing to address your financial concerns directly, as real issues existing in a real world. The final rule of thumb is: if your therapist consistently sees your money concerns as strictly psychological, he may not be able to help you make a wise financial decision *concerning therapy* (though he may still be very helpful on other issues). If this is the case, you should assess your financial motives independently, outside of therapy. On this subject at least, you are on your own.

How do you make this assessment? By casting an appraising eye on your own feelings and actions when it comes to your therapist's fees. The symptoms of a resistance played out in the financial realm include:

- You find yourself thinking *constantly* about the money you are "wasting" on therapy. Maybe you feel that if it weren't for therapy, you would be able to afford all the things you can't now. Maybe you brood continually over how much money your therapist makes. Maybe you tell yourself that if your therapist really cared, he wouldn't be asking you to spend your savings on him, and so forth and so on. Whatever your thoughts, they verge on the obsessive.
- You "act out" when it comes to paying your therapist's bill. You don't pay on time, you forget to sign the check, you are always one or two sessions behind, you frequently devote sessions to trying to renegotiate your fee, and so on.

If either of these descriptions fits you, you may not be ready to leave therapy. So much goes on in therapy that if you are *only* thinking about money, you are probably avoiding other issues. As long as you are investing time and energy in the money issue alone, you are probably still in the grip of your transference. You have not finished working through.

The time to leave therapy is when the subject of your therapist's fees stops being so *fraught*—when it becomes simply one aspect, albeit an important one, of the decision to leave. You are neither obsessed with the money you are spending on therapy *nor* engaged in ongoing fee skirmishes with your therapist, and yet still feel strongly that you are spending too much on treatment. At this point it is time to bring other factors apart from the financial into your decision. The final question isn't only how much is therapy costing you, but how much is therapy costing you *for what you are getting*. If you have done what you came to do, even if you have done only *some* of what you came to do, saving the money you are currently spending on fees may now be a wise decision.

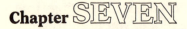

WHEN
IS IT TIME?

Therapy rarely reaches a clear end point. People don't get "cured" in therapy, they just get better (or not). When you are trying to decide whether you are better *enough* to leave therapy, expect to confront both the fact that you still have plenty of problems left and the suspicion that you may be using marginal gains in order to justify not going further for real gains. As Freud wrote in his essay "Analysis Terminable and Interminable":

> Analytic experience has taught us that the better is always the enemy of the good and that in every phase of the patient's recovery we have to fight against his inertia, which is ready to be content with an incomplete solution.

But the issue of when to leave therapy is not as complicated as it may seem. Look around you at others who have left therapy. You probably know at least one person who left before his therapist advised him to (possibly before you would have advised him to your-

124

self, had you been asked). Has he suffered terrible set-backs as a result? Very likely the answer is no. Generally speaking, leaving therapy is not a dire act, nor is leaving therapy too soon.

The Menninger Foundation's massive twenty-year study of forty-two patients in therapy and analysis found that of the twenty-five patients who made either "very good" or "moderate" improvements through therapy, only two backslid after leaving. Since many of these patients left therapy prematurely—in the opinion of their therapists, and sometimes in their own opinion as well—it is clear that leaving too soon is hardly so perilous as it may seem. In fact, some of the patients who left too soon went on to make major life gains outside of therapy. And even the unfortunate pair who left early and "regressed" did not suffer real damage: each one realized he needed further treatment, returned to therapy uneventfully, and afterward made real and lasting progress.

On the basis of this study, it seems fair to conclude that once a typical patient has made real progress of any kind, he or she can safely decide to leave therapy. As for the patient who has *not* made progress, my research indicates that you do not get worse as a result of termination. Of the people I interviewed who did feel that they left therapy prematurely, no one felt it had done him or her any real harm. Instead, they felt certain issues remained—issues they thought they might return to therapy one day in order to deal with.

It seems apparent, then, that the first line of action in approaching this decision is to scale down its psychic dimensions. When the importance of a choice looms out of all proportion, decision-making can be stymied —which in the case of therapy amounts to a de facto decision *not* to leave. This happens to many, many patients. Therapy can stretch on for years while they try

to decide whether it is safe to move on. You should remember as well that leaving therapy too soon is not an
irrevocable decision; it is entirely possible—and productive—simply to go back to therapy if you need to.

And of course, on the other side of the fence there is
the recurring question of whether staying in therapy
too long is actively bad for you. In this respect it is
interesting to note that a number of patients in the
Menninger study made significant improvements *after*
they left therapy. The question is, what would have
happened to these patients had they stayed? Did they
improve *because* they left therapy, or was it simply a
case of therapy having set them on the right track so
that they would continue to progress either inside
treatment or out?

While it is largely impossible to make this judgment
after the fact, in at least one of Wallerstein's cases leaving therapy does seem to have been essential to the patient's improvement. The patient dubbed "Adoptive
Mother" was an infertile married woman whose first
attempt to adopt a child had ended in disaster. After
finding herself gripped by thoughts of harming the
child, she returned the baby to the adoption agency
and checked herself into a mental hospital. Eventually
she arrived at the Menninger Foundation. Therapy
helped, and after leaving therapy she adopted two children successfully. However, she did not adopt until
after she had left therapy. The problem appears to have
been her need for encouragement: she wanted to hear
from her therapist that she would now be able to adopt
a child safely. He was not willing to make her that
guarantee—therapy is not about offering patients assurances that things will now go well. Nevertheless,
Adoptive Mother obviously *needed* assurances, lots of
them. When she left therapy she literally surrounded
herself with support: she depended heavily on her

priest, on a social worker at the adoption agency, and on her medical doctor, who prescribed tranquilizers when she was at her worst. All of these helpers saw her through to an ultimately happy conclusion.

It seems clear that by this point in her life (she was now thirty-one), "Adoptive Mother" needed to begin thinking of herself as emotionally sound and well in order to take an action dependent upon being sound and well. Frequently patients do leave therapy "early" because of their need to feel healthy; feeling mentally sound is a form of self-confidence. Very likely, Adoptive Mother was right to leave therapy when she did, at that point at which continued analysis could have been actually harmful in that it would further have stalled her renewed effort at adoption.

The point is, it can be hard to feel *healthy* as a patient in analysis or therapy. You can feel *secure;* you can feel adequate; you can feel satisfied that you are working seriously on your problems, that you are progressing. But as for feeling that you have *arrived,* that you are not just in transit to a strong and functional you but *there* —that is another story. As many patients have discovered, it is hard to feel that now, as a result of therapy, you are sound, whole, pulled together, ready to take on the world.

In all, leaving therapy too soon rarely appears to be harmful, while leaving therapy too late may be. Given this, at a certain point it begins to make sense to err on the side of leaving rather than on the side of staying.

Different criteria exist for when patients reach this point. First, and easiest to identify, are the *practical* criteria. If you go into therapy with tangible, "objective" goals in mind—like finding a lover or spouse, or making a career shift—you assume it is time to leave when you have achieved these goals.

The only problem with this pragmatic approach to termination is the tendency of some therapists to suggest—or of patients themselves to suspect—that practical, behavioral changes merely treat the "symptoms" without affecting the "disease." This is a sobering thought, since it implies that if you leave therapy you'll shortly find yourself back where you began, all progress erased. The underlying cause of your troubles remains.

Fortunately for anyone grappling with this question, evidence from the Menninger study showed that positive changes of any kind were maintained after termination—and, of course, in many cases patients' lives actually became better still after leaving therapy. A "surface" change is a real change, and a positive surface change is likely to fan out into the rest of your life. If you have finally worked up the nerve, through therapy, to go after and win a better job, you are not going to lose that job because you left therapy. Instead, it is likely that this new job will inspire you with further confidence: change is a kind of therapy in and of itself, and an upward spiral often begins with one significant improvement. If you have been fortunate enough to make real changes in your life through therapy, you owe yourself congratulations, not skepticism.

Of course, even external, "objective" changes can be hard to gauge sometimes—have you really changed, or are you just having a good week? According to many patients and researchers, by the time you have spent a half year in therapy you can trust the changes you have made. Many patients pinpoint a moment about six months along at which they were doing much better, and how long they remained in therapy thereafter had no effect on this progress. In an analysis of 2,400 patients who have been in therapy over the last thirty years, Kenneth I. Howard and his colleagues at North-western University found that typically a patient's *immediate life situation*—such time-bound events as a recent breakup, divorce, or job loss—was significantly improved after six months of therapy. Symptomatic relief occurs even faster. Within four or five *sessions,* says Howard, a patient's symptoms of distress—nervousness, tension, problems eating or sleeping—are usually alleviated.

Changing more deep-seated patterns is another matter, at least according to Howard. He sees a real difference between a patient who has had problems relating to women since his divorce and a patient who has always had problems relating to women. For the thirty-five-year-old man who has never had a relationship with a woman, a six-month stint in therapy is probably not going to be enough. Howard suggests an intriguing rule: improvement is a logarithmic function of the number of sessions a patient attends. Put simply, this means that after a certain point in treatment, in order to see any further improvement at all the patient would have to *double* the length of time he spends in treatment. In therapy, six months is a key period, after which you should expect to spend a year for further improvement. If a year is insufficient you probably need two. And so on. (This is the same principle physicians use in prescribing drugs. If a 2.5 mg dose of Valium does not bring relief, the doctor doubles the dose to 5 mg, and after that to 10 mg, then finally to 20.)

Once you have alleviated your immediate life situation in the first six months, it could take years really to make a dent in long-standing destructive habits. Therefore, the six-month point is a good time to assess whether or not you should remain in therapy. If you were suffering from a particular setback when you entered therapy, by now you have probably come to grips with it. This does not necessarily mean that you have solved your problem, but that you feel you are in control of your life once again. You can *cope* with whatever is ahead. And now may be the time to leave. Diminishing returns are going to set in; each extra month will bring less progress than did the initial six. Any further changes in habits, conflicts, or longtime personality patterns will probably take another six months at least, and quite possibly two years or more. If you have not improved your lot at all in six months, you can decide to give therapy another six months, or you may choose to change therapists.

At least, this is the course Dr. Howard's findings suggest. However, there is considerable disagreement among therapists as to the nature, degree, and speed at which deeper, more sweeping character change can occur. Two schools of thought exist. Howard leans toward the view that major changes simply do not happen, years of therapy or no. He offers chronic loneliness as an example of a problem that even extended therapy will not budge. If you went into therapy because you have always been lonely, he says, you are likely to stay lonely. You can remain in therapy for life trying to change this reality. Howard lists standard "predictors" that signal a therapy that will have no end: for example, the patient is a woman in her thirties, living alone, with no significant relationships—neither friends nor lovers—who comes in complaining of loneliness. A patient with this profile, says Howard, is likely to stay in therapy for good—and to stay lonely for good as well.

Other researchers take a more optimistic view. The Menninger study offers at least one case history that provides evidence to the contrary: the six-year treatment of a patient called "English Professor." By the time he sought help, English Professor was in such a bad way that he was dismissing classes early, avoiding his friends, and spending all his free time driving the town alone and insulated in his car. At age thirty-five, he had never had a stable relationship with a woman. Finally his situation deteriorated so completely that he quit his job and had himself hospitalized.

Six years of therapy resulted in sweeping change. English Professor was able to make a home of his own, to hold a job and earn tenure, to marry, and even finally to have a child. He published extensively—another area of "phobic inhibition" prior to analysis—ending his career as a "fairly well-noted expert in his field of specialization." From total paralysis, both sexual and professional, he went to a new life as a successful professor and family man. He *changed*.

Psychologists and psychiatrists commonly make a distinction between "behavioral" and "structural" change. Behavioral change is precisely what it sounds like: alterations in surface behaviors like going out on dates where before you stayed home, or sending out letters and résumés where once you merely read the classifieds. Structural change is much more difficult to define. Roughly, it is change in the set of basic character traits, defenses, and conflicts that cause a person to act the way he does. Traditionally, most experts have agreed that structural change goes deeper, takes longer, and ultimately lasts longer once it occurs. For years therapists have held that structural change is superior to behavioral change, which has been dismissed as merely that: behavioral.

While behavioral change is relatively easy to recognize—your friends can tell you whether you are acting differently, if you don't know—structural change is less obvious and consequently harder to assess. The easiest criterion to use here is to ask yourself whether or not you have made any changes in your standard defense mechanisms. Defense mechanisms are basic parts of personality, so any alteration in them amounts to true structural change. In assessing whether or not you have made structural change, ask yourself whether you have altered your characteristic way of dealing with threats to your self-esteem—threats from the inside as well as from the outside.

David, a man who saw a therapist for four years, is a good example of a person who altered his standard way of coping with problems. Before therapy he had always exercised "denial": for David, bad things—either in the world or in himself—simply were not real. David's practice of denial was so ingrained that it led to some real problems in his life. At work he had been oblivious to the fact that by taking too visible credit for the success of a recent project he had alienated his immediate superior. At home his denial caused tension with his wife because David saw himself as one who could do no wrong. His unconscious mind simply denied the existence of any possible bad motive or wrongdoing on his part.

After four years of therapy, David had taken off the blinders: he could see—and head off—trouble in the professional realm, and he could acknowledge and apologize for his own role in any problems with his wife. (Whether or not a full four years were necessary is an open question; however, David does feel that six months of therapy would not have been sufficient to alter this basic aspect of his character.) David continues to be expert at denial in a positive sense: he frequently is able to dismiss the reality of painful situations he can't do anything about. What therapy has done for David is to strip away the negative, immature aspects of denial, leaving him with its strength.

David's transformed version of denial stood him in

good stead when he and his wife later had trouble conceiving a child. Throughout their year of seeing doctors and undergoing tests he simply did not believe they could truly have a problem. Even after a real, physical problem—one that proved easily correctable—had been diagnosed, he remained unswerving in his belief that they would have a child. "There's nothing really wrong with you," he told his wife one day as she despaired of ever having a baby. Meaning: "There's something *slightly* wrong with you that can be fixed. I'm not worried." This is healthy denial; it has lost its neurotic component.

George Vaillant, M.D., has usefully summarized the defense mechanisms for the *Harvard Medical School Mental Health Letter*. He begins with the "psychotic" defenses, moving through the "immature" to "neurotic" defenses and finally to "mature" defenses. Under immature defenses he includes:

- Projection: You attribute your own "bad" feelings to others.
- Hypochondria: Annoyance with others turns first into annoyance with yourself and then into exaggerated physical complaints.
- Passive Aggression: You express hostility passively—for example, by "forgetting" to run a crucial errand your spouse was depending on you to do.
- Acting Out: You express an unconscious wish or conflict through actions (often negative) in order to avoid having to deal with it consciously—for example, by having an extramarital affair when what you are really feeling is anger toward your spouse.

The neurotic defenses are:

- Denial: You avoid upset by unconsciously denying the reality of a distressing situation.

- Intellectualization: You divorce all feeling from a heavily emotional topic, thinking about it in purely rational terms.
- Repression: You push something that disturbs you out of consciousness—though often the *feeling* remains conscious while the thoughts and images associated with it "disappear."
- Displacement: You transfer disturbing feelings and thoughts from their "rightful" object to a second, less important object; for example, a graduate student coming up to her oral examinations might spend her days and nights obsessively worrying about her love life instead of the test.
- Reaction Formation: You have intense conscious feelings and thoughts that directly oppose the dangerous impulse you are defending against—the classic heavy-drinker-turned-temperance-preacher mechanism.

What makes these defenses immature or neurotic is that they are ways of enabling you to avoid reality. By contrast, the mature defenses take all aspects of a painful situation or conflict into account, and cope with the problem on that basis. These mature defenses include:

- Altruism: You give generously to others to gratify an instinct, sometimes through a vicarious gratification.
- Humor: Forbidden wishes or impulses are expressed through humor that harms neither you nor someone else.
- Suppression: Unlike the case of denial or repression, you *consciously* decide not to think about something painful.
- Anticipation: You consider how you're going to react to an expected difficulty.
- Sublimation: You express any antisocial impulses in socially acceptable ways—a classic Freudian concept.

Consider these definitions if you are trying to decide whether you have accomplished a structural change. If you find that you now rely more on the mature defenses than on the less mature ones with which you came to therapy, then you have made a significant change. And you are certainly in good shape to leave.

Structural change also occurs in the resolution of a patient's neurotic conflicts. "Adoptive Mother" was thought by her doctors to be suffering from conflicts that specifically concerned her mother, who was both highly devoted and highly controlling. Mother and daughter had never been close, though both were united in shared hostility toward the father, who was improvident and alcoholic, and suffered from a venereal disease. The result of this family constellation was a daughter torn between anger at, and identification with, her mother—a conflict that occasioned other conflicts over femininity and motherhood. Her analysts felt the "core" conflict concerning her mother was the basis of her problems with adoption. Resolve the conflict, and the adoption struggle would be resolved as well.

In reality, Adoptive Mother did not resolve these conflicts, and yet she was able to adopt an infant anyway. This brings us to the issue of whether basic conflicts ever do get resolved—or, in fact, whether they need to be. Freud originally set out to help patients resolve conflicts, but by the end of his life he no longer believed conflicts could be resolved once and for all; while you could get a particular conflict under control in particular circumstances, there was no guarantee that future versions of it would not be aroused by future events. Ultimately he came to believe that the point of psychoanalysis was not the eradication of conflicts but the taming of the instincts that produced them in the first place.

Many modern theorists agree. Psychoanalyst Arnold Z. Pfeffer offered one of the more affecting formulations of this position when he wrote that the real goal of therapy is not to banish the conflict forever but to make it *lose its poignancy.* The conflict remains, but it is less intense—and more conscious as well. When conflict-arousing situations threaten, the patient is able to see them coming and handle them, or ward them off altogether.

In short, psychically the patient remains who he is. A woman raised by a controlling mother and a diseased, alcoholic father does not achieve the mental makeup of a woman raised by loving parents who got on well in life. The hoped-for outcome of therapy is best expressed by Freud himself, speaking of one of his own patients: "An analysis lasting three-quarters of a year...restored to the patient, an excellent and worthy person, her right to a share in life." This is the true goal of therapy: to reach the point at which past troubles and hurts no longer hold you back.

Must you undergo structural change in order to claim your own right to a share in life? The Menninger study concluded that the traditional distinction between structural change achieved through analysis of conflicts, and behavioral change achieved through the therapist's support and encouragment, is false. Behavioral change is *real* change, and lasts just as long. Furthermore, behavioral change seems also to *include* structural change: when patients at Menninger changed their behavior, they often modified underlying conflicts and defenses as well. In short, behavioral change is a major accomplishment, and to some extent behavioral change *is* structural change.

Because behavioral changes are external, observable

events, they make judging whether you are ready to leave therapy much easier. While it is difficult in the extreme to gauge how "resolved" you are, it is a much simpler matter to know whether or not you are getting along better with your husband. Almost anyone can tell you whether you're conducting your life more productively now than when you went into therapy—including yourself. But when you believe that the only correct standard for termination is structural change, you may feel that your therapist is the best judge. Deciding whether your core conflict is resolved, or if your defense structure is altered, are questions on which even trained analysts will disagree. It is genuinely hard to know. All told, when making a decision to terminate, it is better to hold to behavioral standards of change.

Assuming constructive behavioral change is your goal, how long *should* it take? Kenneth Howard offers one answer: six months for the immediate, life-crisis problems; years for habits of long standing.

However, experiments with "short-term" therapy offer promising evidence that even long-term difficulties can sometimes yield to therapy in a short period of time. Strupp's short-term program at Vanderbilt University is particularly interesting because he and his colleagues clearly address patients' long-standing conflicts. Of course, Strupp himself does not claim to work miracles. He cautions that the patients most likely to be successful in short-term therapy—in any therapy, for that matter—are those who are healthiest going in. A longtime pattern of "failure in living," says Strupp, lowers the chances of major improvement considerably. But he goes on to present encouraging case histories of patients who do, in fact, seem to have worked through, in a very short time, problems and personality patterns that have been hampering them for years.

This change takes place in an average of twenty-four sessions, meeting once weekly for approximately six months (again, the six-month stretch).

Apart from the time limitation, Strupp's approach, "Time-Limited Dynamic Psychotherapy" (TLDP), applies the principles of classic psychodynamic therapy with some modifications. For Strupp and his colleagues the transference relationship is key, with the therapist using his own countertransference as a clue to the patient's characteristic modes of functioning. Beyond this, TLDP parts ways with long-term psychodynamic therapy in two important respects. In TLDP therapists focus heavily on the patient's present life. The goal is *not* to sift through the patient's childhood, but to understand exactly what is going wrong in the present and what to do about it. In part, this focus is dictated by the brevity of treatment: there isn't time, in twenty-four sessions, to delve into a patient's youth. But Strupp also makes the convincing argument that memory, in any event, is a *reconstruction*—which means that what you remember inside therapy about your childhood is often different from what you remember outside of therapy about your childhood. Moreover, both "memories" are different from what your childhood actually *was*. In short, the way you recall your childhood is simply one more aspect of your transference. In TLDP therapists go straight after the transference by analyzing present-time transferential action and feeling.

TLDP also differs from conventional long-term therapy in Strupp's use of what he calls the "dynamic focus." Basically, the dynamic focus is to a person what a thesis is to a book: it is a central, unifying *theme* that runs through almost everything one says and does in relation to other people. Strupp's "dynamic focus" includes four basic categories of information: how the patient feels and acts; how the patient expects others to react to him; how others actually do act toward the patient; and how the patient acts toward himself. Of course, all therapists examine these issues, but what is unique about TLDP is that all of this information is organized and unified into one coherent central proposition concerning the patient's life—a central proposition the patient, as well as the therapist, can hold on to.

The "focal theme" of a career woman in her late thirties, married with two children, who came to short-term therapy at Vanderbilt complaining of an anxiety and depression she had been feeling for years is as follows:

> I must be a good girl, not experience anger toward significant men (husband, father, therapist), and do their bidding. Unless I do, they may leave me, withdraw their love, abandon me. I can prevent separation—and the disturbing feeling of loss—by acting right. By implication, too, whatever may go wrong in a relationship, it is my fault and it is my responsibility to prevent such occurrences.

This theme, arrived at by *both* patient and therapist working together, makes therapy efficient in the extreme. As her therapy was to show, most of this woman's difficulties—such as not speaking openly to her husband about problems and being overly critical of her children—did in fact stem from this privately held scenario. Now other material she brought in could be understood—and dealt with—from the perspective of her focal theme.

Compare this one unifying "focal theme" to the multiple themes developed in the course of "Adoptive Mother's" three-year analysis:

1) her unhappiness derived from wanting a child but not feeling able to have one
2) the feeling of not getting what she wanted out of treatment
3) the feeling of being the innocent little child who does not understand what is going on
4) the deep yearning for closeness, which had to be simultaneously pushed off
5) the need to dominate and control the treatment and the therapist in the service of her assertive and aggressive strivings
6) the closely related severe and basic problem of her sexual identity and her manifest penis envy
7) the constant theme of having to choose between husband and analyst
8) her desire to be a small child
9) her desire that the analyst be her lover
10) the doubts about the strength of her religious convictions
11) the similar doubts about whether she could ever believe in or love her husband or ever be a good wife to him

With its eleven separate themes, even at the level of simple memory this list is overwhelming—*true,* but overwhelming. Organization and coherence are powerful mental principles, and TLDP's use of a focal theme puts these basic cognitive principles to use. In any given situation, "Career Woman" can readily remember her one basic theme and apply it. If, say, she is feeling silent resentment toward her husband for not doing his share of the housework, she can remind herself that in the past she has not voiced resentment for fear of angering a man who mattered to her—and in this case she is on the verge of doing precisely the same thing. Having silently reviewed her focal theme as it applies to this new situation, she can presumably choose to act differently, however difficult that may be.

Over the course of Career Woman's twenty-seven sessions her focal theme turned up again and again within the transference. Each time, she and her therapist would analyze how her theme had played itself out on this new occasion, and then would extend their insight to other aspects of her life. By the end of therapy she and her therapist had so thoroughly established her theme that she could not help but spot it whenever it occurred.

Career Woman's life continued to change after she left therapy. Ten months after terminating she returned for one follow-up appointment to report that she had continued to make progress. She was now talking to her husband openly about problems; he was now sharing the housework; she had become less sensitive to criticism from him. She had become more sexually responsive as well. With her children she was now much less impatient; with her mother she was more tolerant. Finally, she had grown much more confident and assertive at work, taking on responsibilities she would not have felt comfortable shouldering before therapy. In all, an impressive array of change—all accomplished as a result of a mere twenty-seven sessions.

And Career Woman had made structural as well as behavioral change. Some therapists hold that any change in a recurring dream is an indication of structural change. Career Woman had had a recurring dream concerning a man twenty years her senior with whom she had been involved years before. Ultimately, she had decided not to marry him, but for some years she had dreamed that she found herself longing for a reconciliation with him. About ten months after termination, this dream changed. She dreamed of him again, but now it was he who wanted the reconciliation, while she herself felt distant. This change was so striking, in fact, that it prompted her to call for the follow-up ap-

pointment. Her therapist interpreted the dream as signaling that she was less focused upon her father (who
had died while she was in college) and ready to grow
closer to her husband. She was, in Strupp's words, "de-
lighted with this idea," as well she should have been.

Career Woman's success suggests that short-term therapy is a viable alternative. But those already engaged
in long-term therapy and wondering whether to leave
should take into consideration the following:

- An immediate crisis can often be handled in six
  months, and the immediate symptoms you came in
  with in a few sessions.
- Small changes are real changes. If you feel satisfied
  with the level of change you have achieved, you are
  right to leave.
- Long-standing problems are tougher and, according to
  some (though not all) therapists, may take longer to
  change. Even so, you should take stock of where you
  are within at least one year's time. If your negative
  patterns have not changed, I recommend finding a
  new therapist.

Of course, in recent years we have seen a good deal of
published pessimism concerning the effectiveness of
therapy, with some professionals arguing that people
cannot really change all that much no matter how
many therapists they see. Dr. Howard is a persuasive
voice here, as is Bernie Zilbergeld, author of *The
Shrinking of America*. Neither author believes that
great change can be wrought through therapy; people
pretty much are who they are. No amount of therapy
will turn a shy person into a raging extrovert, or a
chronically lonely one into a social trend-setter.

No doubt both men are right, but the question is:
does this matter? How much personal change do peo-

ple actually seek? For example, do shy people really want to move center stage? It would seem not. In my interviews I did not encounter a single person who wished to be transformed into his opposite number. What people want instead is to become happier and more productive versions of what they already are.

This goal therapy seems well equipped to handle, through the steady accumulation of small change. As our case histories show, a few small changes in the heart and mind of one person soon become a welcome new beginning. Ultimately the distinction between modest and grand, between "behavioral" and "structural," comes to seem unimportant. Small changes are important changes; they are changes that matter.

If you have made small changes, if moreover you have acquired the knack for continuing to make small changes, your therapy has been a success. It may be time to try setting out on your own; certainly you are not going to fall on your face if you do.

If on the other hand nothing is happening, no changes large or small, you must find a new therapist. The Menninger study includes a few patients who finally improved after going through as many as three different therapists—evidence of the importance of connecting with the right person. Therapy helps so many people that if it is not working at all for you there is a strong likelihood you are matched up with the wrong therapist. Finally, if you have already changed therapists over the years with no real improvement, then the only reason to stay is the day-to-day quality of your therapy sessions. If they add to your life, if you *want* to go on, then do. If not, you should consider the possibility that therapy has become part of the problem. If that is the case, it is time to leave.

LEAVE-TAKING

By and large, termination, even a "good" termination, hurts. Termination is saying goodbye—no one's favorite exchange. A good termination is therefore handled with delicacy. Typically the patient, not the therapist, has raised the issue of leaving. The therapist usually has a feel for whether his patient seriously wants to leave or is merely expressing some form of resistance. Dr. Sonya Rhodes of Manhattan believes therapists should take any mention of termination seriously, to prevent them from misinterpreting a genuine desire to leave as mere transference. She suggests that a patient who is thinking of leaving take time off to see how it goes. The ball, as the saying goes, is then in the patient's court.

Responding to a patient's expressed wish to leave is a difficult issue for therapists because many patients—perhaps all patients at one point or another—speak of leaving when they don't really want to. This is a standard form of resistance. Furthermore, bringing up termination prematurely can be a form of *rehearsal*, one of the mature defense mechanisms. Given the finite na-

144

ture of therapy, it makes emotional sense to anticipate its termination, to rehearse it beforehand, and broaching the subject in session is a good way to do so.

It is a fact of life for therapists that patients will bring up the prospect of termination, and bring it up often. Usually the therapist initially resists the move, while his patient continues to insist. Often the therapist is right to resist; when he is wrong, a good therapist will readily revise his opinion. Your role, when you have truly decided to leave, is to keep bringing the subject up until your therapist sees that you are in earnest, particularly if you have sounded false alarms about leaving in the past. It is up to you to communicate the fact that this time you mean it.

There are two common approaches to terminating therapy, but the general consensus within the profession runs *against* "weaning" and *for* setting a date. Weaning means that the patient tapers off by cutting back on the number and frequency of sessions. Many patients would prefer to terminate therapy this way, and some therapists allow it. But most therapists feel that weaning allows the patient to avoid dealing with the reality that therapy truly is coming to an end. When you simply trail off rather than totally stop, you avoid the goodbye—and avoid confronting the feelings associated with it.

Setting a date for the final session soon after termination is under way makes it *real*. Establishing an actual, identifiable, circle-it-on-your-calendar date forces the issue; the patient cannot so easily evade the fact that a separation is in the offing. He is forced to deal with his feelings. And many therapists have found that some of the most productive work of therapy occurs *during* termination, under the pressure of the coming end. It is not that new material comes up; rather, old material takes on new shape. This may be the strongest argument of all against never-ending therapy. If you never terminate, you never go through termination. Most therapists believe the termination period should last several months; periods of a year are not uncommon when the therapy has lasted some years already.

The tasks of termination fall into two categories: often intensified work on major issues and new work specifically on the twin issues of separation and loss. Separation is a universal concern; some theorists go so far as to claim it is the fundamental issue of all therapy. And termination is the phase of therapy that addresses this issue most directly.

Because separation is so powerful a concern, patients seem to fare best when their therapists do *not* impose a strict end to all contact. Patients subjected to the cold-turkey approach—*now you're out of therapy for good*—often find their terminations unsatisfactory. An "open-door" policy is preferable. Some therapists tell departing patients they can return if they need to; one woman reports that her psychiatrist kept the hour of her session open until he was sure she was not returning. Other therapists say they would like to hear from their patients from time to time; still others suggest a more formal checkup six months or so after termination. However the sentiment is phrased, the point is made that the therapist will still be there.

Volunteering this reassurance is in itself a final act of generosity on the part of the therapist. A departing patient needs to feel strong; it is not good to be constantly in touch with your vulnerability when you are taking a vulnerable step. Therapists who freely offer reassurance allow their patients not to feel their *need* for reassurance, at least not as much as they would if they had to ask for it. These therapists gladly put their patients in a position of strength, and by making it possible for a patient to come back, they make it possible for him not to come back. Absolute loss is traumatic. The open door renders your loss leaving therapy no less *real*, only less calamitous.

Finally, in a good termination the therapist gives his "blessing." He volunteers his belief that the patient is ready, that now is a good time to terminate the therapy. In offering his approval, the therapist effectively lets go of his patient, giving him "permission" to leave. This is important, because if your therapist continues to argue against your leaving up to the bitter end (and these cases can become bitter indeed), you are forced into a defiant stance. In order to leave, you must rebel. You have no choice but to decide you know better than your therapist. Until now you have trusted your therapist to be *right;* that is partly the basis of the therapeutic alliance. Once your therapist has taken the position that you should stay, you are forced to declare him flat-out wrong in order to justify going, thus calling into question the entire history of your relationship with him. Has he been wrong before? Influenced by bad motives? What has really been going on?

Such a sequence of advancing disillusionment amounts to a major psychic upheaval, one that is much more disruptive than it might immediately seem. Parting in the midst of a disagreement is quite different from parting when you see eye to eye; you suffer not just loss but, essentially, a breakup as well. This is hard, because no agreement can be reached, no sense of resolution achieved. At best you can only agree to disagree, and an agreement to disagree is seldom a satisfactory ending. Unavoidably, you leave with unfinished business.

There is also the simple matter of how you feel after the last session. A good termination is like a good grad-

uation: it is an achievement, an arrival, a second coming-of-age. When your therapist balks, he deprives you
of that feeling of pride in what you have accomplished.

The final session itself poses a dilemma for patient and
therapist both: what is supposed to happen here? More
therapy? Or is it simply an opportunity to say, "So
long, it's been good to know you"? Many patients do
not appreciate having their final gestures subjected to
analysis. To take one commonplace example, when
your therapist asks you to examine exactly *why* you
have brought him a parting gift, it rankles. And for
good reason: the final session is the bridge between
being a patient and not being a patient. It is the last
station in your journey from one condition to another,
from not happy to happier, from "neurotic" to healthy.
A good termination is a *passage*, and the final session
should confirm that you have made that passage.

How does the therapist acknowledge his patient's
new strength? Often by taking the direct route: he may
simply say, "You have done well." *We* have done well.
One significant action the therapist can take is to re-
frain from treating his patient's final gestures as symptoms. Steve, a graphic artist, in parting drew a picture
for his analyst on the back of his final bill. His therapist, who was using every argument in the book to persuade Steve not to go (this after many years of analysis), adamantly refused to accept the gift unless Steve
agreed to analyze why he had given it to him. In this
situation the therapist's interpretive stance amounted
to little more than a ploy; he was angling to turn
Steve's goodbye into yet another symptom signaling
the need for yet more therapy. He was trying to maneuver Steve back into the patient position.

Even a therapist who agrees with his patient's desire

to leave can make this misstep. At the end of her final session Marta wanted to hug her therapist goodbye. His response: to suggest she ask herself why a hug. This is not the best note on which to end. While it may be true that any action has its hidden motives, in "normal" life we agree to ignore this analytic precept. Society simply could not function smoothly if at every turn secretaries were saying to bosses, and mothers were saying to children, and lovers were saying to lovers, "I wonder what you *really* mean by that." Life outside therapy does not—*cannot*—run this way. And the final session of therapy is, in fact, a release back into real life. In the last session a therapist who is truly letting go usually (though not always) refrains from analyzing his patient's way of taking leave. He or she takes the patient's goodbye as just that: a goodbye and a thank-you.

On the other hand, saying goodbye is always hard, and part of what the therapist who analyzes his patient's goodbye is doing is simply making the goodbye less final. He is saying, in effect, "You're still my patient, I'm still your therapist. Don't worry." There is also the fact that the patient is paying for this final session; to some extent the therapist has to be still doing therapy in order to justify the final fee.

Phoebe can attest to this. A thirty-one-year-old woman who had been in therapy for six months, she found herself feeling quite irritated during the last session when her therapist shifted into an everyday chatty mode; Phoebe was very money-conscious, and she did not want to pay seventy-five dollars just to hear goodbye and good luck. As she puts it, "I wanted every second to *count.*"

Even so, her final session is a good prototype for this manner of ending. Phoebe had gone into therapy to try to make a decision about having children. She was profoundly ambivalent over the prospect and could not come to a resolution on her own. Her therapy uncovered the reason for her conflict: as a child she had been repeatedly molested by a neighbor boy only three years her senior, and she had felt intense guilt about it ever since. The adult fallout of this childhood trauma was a terror of having children—especially little girls—who would themselves be vulnerable to hurt.

Having come to this realization (something that happened in a short six months, confirming Dr. Howard's findings), Phoebe now felt ready to leave. Although she had not decided whether she would have children, she believed she had cleared the way to do so. Her therapist agreed; in fact, she went so far as to say that she had never seen a patient make so much progress in so little time as had Phoebe. It was a real vote of confidence, and the kind of thing patients need to hear.

Phoebe's idea of leaving, like most patients', was simply to leave, to say, "I won't be back next week." But her therapist objected. A formal termination was essential, she said. While Phoebe found her therapist's justifications for a formal termination vague, her therapist had been right so many times before that Phoebe went along.

At this point her therapist made a slight misstep. She did not suggest they set an official termination date. Phoebe now found herself trying—unsuccessfully—to work up the courage each session to designate the *next* session as the last. Fortunately for her, a job offer in another city intervened, and the date was set according to Phoebe's scheduled move. She is not sure what would have happened otherwise; she does not have the impression that her therapist, left to her own devices, would ever have suggested a date.

Whatever the truth of the matter, this limbo state

lasted only a couple of weeks, during which Phoebe and her therapist did not cover any important material—unlike many other cases, in which patients do some of their most significant work during the closing months and weeks of therapy. When the last session arrived, Phoebe had very mixed feelings about it. She did not like paying to say goodbye; in addition, she felt "corny." She had worked hard at not making her therapist into a friend, at not coming to feel she would need her therapist forever, and had therefore maintained a professional attitude: You are my doctor, I am your patient. To have a session expressly devoted to the quintessentially emotional business of saying goodbye seemed to breach this professionalism. After all, as she pointed out, you don't go out of your way to say goodbye to your gynecologist; her last pelvic exam had come and gone with no fond farewell. Besides, all goodbyes are difficult, and Phoebe had to fight a strong impulse to skip this one altogether, a common reaction among patients. The prospect of a formal, fifty-minute parting is daunting to say the least. Probably the majority of patients feel a real urge not to show that last day.

Phoebe resisted that urge, and her last session was quite different in tone and content from the sessions of the previous six months. No analysis or interpretation occurred; instead Phoebe and her therapist talked "trivia," as Phoebe puts it. They spoke about Phoebe's upcoming job, about the move, about how Lou (Phoebe's husband, who would be staying behind to remain at his own job for the time being) was going to handle the separation. And for the first time ever, Phoebe's therapist offered direct advice. She told Phoebe that she and Lou should make sure to see each other every other weekend, that they needed at least that minimal amount of time together. That final piece of advice made a real impression on both Phoebe and her husband, and they did, in fact, set up an every-other-week schedule that they held to over the next months until Phoebe's husband was able to find a job near hers.

According to Stephen K. Firestein, M.D., author of *Termination in Psychoanalysis*, giving advice is a common reaction to termination among therapists. Facing the end of their time with a patient, therapists grow worried about all the ground they have not covered—or have not covered sufficiently—and often become much more directive as a result. Since there is no time left, the therapist begins simply to *tell* the patient things the patient has not yet figured out for himself.

At her session's end Phoebe did not know what move to make, whether to hug her therapist or not. Finally she did nothing. The two women rose and walked out to the reception area, where one more parting scene took place: saying goodbye to the receptionist. Phoebe found this exchange somewhat unnerving because the receptionist had always been very professional. Typically she made cheery, upbeat small talk with patients waiting for their appointments, and there was never any reference to the fact that they were *patients* who were presumably there to discuss *problems*. When Phoebe's therapist announced to the receptionist that "Phoebe is leaving us," Phoebe felt strange indeed. Suddenly the (obvious) fact that she was there for therapy was being spoken out loud, and she was being congratulated and wished luck by therapist and secretary alike.

Clearly, this therapist's efforts at normalcy were not quite coming off. Even so, though it felt awkward to Phoebe it *did* work as a successful passage. Phoebe describes her last day as feeling like a graduation, what with the wishes for luck in the future and the final goodbyes. It was a send-off. When Phoebe reached her car, she felt elated mainly, she says, for having survived the goodbyes, about which she had been very nervous. But it is fair to suspect that some of her emotion came from the warm and positive farewell. The next week, when her usual hour for therapy arrived, she felt happy and also a little sad at the same time. She missed therapy some, but she really was finished. And her therapist's handling of the final session had helped her *feel* finished. That last session, complete with its goodbye to the staff, had given Phoebe a sense of, in her word, "closure."

On leaving therapy certain emotions are universal— grief and anxiety, as well as excitement over the coming change with all its possibilities. Most patients hope to see their therapists again sometime in the future, and many concoct fantasies of running into their therapists by chance in some "normal" setting—a party, say. Some take this impulse to the extent of wishing to form a friendship with their therapist after the therapeutic relationship has ended.

Often patients wish they could leave "early," i.e., without waiting until the official termination date. The reasons are obvious. If you leave today you don't have to spend the next six months *talking* about leaving— and experiencing all the painful emotions that accompany talking about leaving. Also, in leaving early a patient seizes the initiative, so to speak; that is, he avoids the additional hurt of experiencing a loss "passively." He is *doing* the leaving, not just undergoing it. Firestein reports that many patients experience termination more profoundly, as a kind of rebirth, which often takes a vicarious form; departing patients (men and women both) decide to have babies themselves or are suddenly flooded with sadness that they have not had one in the past.

In addition, initial symptoms frequently reappear, along with initial modes of resistance. If your initial way of reacting to your therapist was, say, to refuse for long stretches of time to speak to him, you may find yourself doing the same thing all over again. You may find old symptoms ominously reappearing outside therapy. If, for example, you came into therapy because of work problems (such as procrastination and passivity), and suddenly you find yourself procrastinating and growing passive again, you may panic.

You shouldn't. Therapists do not see such recurrences as serious. Instead they interpret these regressions as last-ditch attempts to hold on to therapy. The patient is saying, in effect, "I'm not ready to go"—even though in fact he is. In Firestein's study of eight patients terminating analysis, all such regression was short-lived: no one was truly returning to his or her old ways. Not only do these regressions quickly subside, but typically the therapeutic alliance grows much stronger and more productive during the formal termination period.

A number of less obvious reactions to termination are common as well. One to guard against in particular is displaced anger. At some level, many patients feel angry that therapy is ending. Even though it is you who have made the decision to go, you can nonetheless feel abandoned when your therapist agrees. But instead of getting mad at your therapist (whom you are about to lose "forever"), you get mad at your spouse (who is going to stick around). Suddenly you may find yourself unnaturally irritated with your spouse (or lover or close friends) over trivial matters that normally would not faze you. This is displaced anger, anger redirected to a safe target. Alternatively, you may find yourself feeling fine in therapy but not able to function so well at home or at work. Again, this is probably a result of the stress of leaving therapy, transferred to other realms. It will pass.

Another standard response to termination is to devalue your entire therapeutic experience. As the final session draws near, you may find yourself turning sour on therapy, feeling it has not been worth the time or the money. While in some cases these opinions may be valid, when they come on suddenly during termination they are suspect. Many patients feel a keen sense of disappointment when they realize, now that therapy is about to end, that they truly are not going to become perfect, and perfectly happy, beings. As long as therapy goes on, a patient can maintain the hope—the fantasy —of fixing everything, but when the final date is set reality inevitably sinks in. If you find yourself suddenly rejecting your entire therapy experience as pointless you may be reacting painfully to the fact that there are limits to what you have accomplished. Moreover, devaluing therapy is a deft way of diminishing the pain of separation: your therapy (and therapist) was never any good anyway, so why should you care that it is over?

The common eleventh-hour fantasy of *becoming* an analyst is interpreted as another form of holding on. If you become a therapist yourself, you stay with your therapist forever, since you are now part of him, part of his profession. In the most concrete version of this scenario, the patient sees himself becoming an actual colleague of his therapist, thereby ensuring that the two will remain in contact forever. There may be a second factor at work here as well: becoming a therapist is a way of becoming your therapist's equal, of leaving patient status behind. The patient can use this image of himself as therapist to rehearse the impending change in his status and role.

Another way to sustain the tie to your therapist is to avoid paying the final bill. Lives there the therapist who has not had to move heaven and earth to collect a final payment from a patient who, until now, has been entirely reliable about sending checks? The number of patients who have trouble parting with that last sum is legion, even though many of them realize exactly what they are doing, and why. Some patients have gone as long as two years before finally sending off the last check.

Finally, many, many patients wish to leave their analyst with some token of their gratitude, a gift. Again, the customary analytic interpretation is that this gesture is a means of leaving some part of yourself with your therapist for good. Your gift, in this view, represents yourself. Part of you stays behind.

Marta's experience with terminating therapy is an example of the way the process should be handled. A former nurse who is now a full-time mother and homemaker, Marta first entered therapy in a state of extreme distress. She was barely holding herself together through a relentless procession of losses, each coming directly upon the other's heels: first the deaths of her father and, shortly after, her mother, then the selling of her childhood home, then the discovery that her husband was infertile. She was devastated.

She turned to therapy for help, and stayed four and a half years. Her termination took up the final twelve months, a period marked by a great deal of back-and-forth. Marta would announce that she did not need to come back again after that day's session; her therapist would caution that leaving therapy took planning; then she would dutifully agree to return for one session more. Altogether, he "held her back"—to use her words —for a full six months. At the time she found this frustrating and would tell him so. "I feel like a bird that is having its wings clipped," she said often. In retrospect she strongly believes he was right; she needed the extra time.

On the other hand, as strongly as Marta was pressing to terminate, she did not want to leave altogether. What she proposed was to cut back to a once-monthly schedule, which she planned to stay with indefinitely. This her therapist would not agree to. He told her that leaving therapy had to be a definite act, a real decision and a real departure. Because she trusted him, she accepted this opinion on faith.

Finally, about two months before she actually left, her therapist told her she was ready to go. In effect, he gave her permission to leave, as well as a much-welcomed endorsement. Together they set the end of January as the date, choosing this time because it would be one month after a plane trip Marta planned to take. She suffered from fear of flying, and in her mind the trip amounted to a test; she would be taking with her on the flight a bottle of tranquilizers her therapist had prescribed for her, as a symbol of his necessary presence in her life.

On the flight she did not actually take any pills, and when she felt bold enough to throw them away, she knew it was a sign that she was definitely leaving therapy. She saw her therapist for the final month, and then said goodbye. Leave-taking was painful; she cried a lot working up to it, and she cried in her car afterward, though she got through the session itself with dry eyes.

In the final session Marta talked about how hard it was to leave. She wanted to hug her therapist; he responded by asking her to think about this: why a hug *in particular?* While it might have been better form on his part simply to accept a hug—or to accept the sentiment that made her want to give him one—he was quite gracious when Marta sent him a cartoon she had cut out from the paper along with her final payment. He did not analyze her gift. Instead he called to thank her and to ask how she was doing. She was well.

In spite of how smoothly her leave-taking went, some months later Marta still does not feel she is entirely "over" her termination, nor does she expect she ever will be. She fully anticipates she will always feel a special connection with her therapist, and a special sense of loss as well—as she probably should. Marta had known her therapist for four and a half years, and he had seen her through profound life crises. For years she had depended on his support and insight, on his being there, and he always was.

Leaving group therapy falls into a category of its own. Group satisfies more of your social needs than does individual therapy, and it is correspondingly more complicated to leave. With group not only do you have a therapist to listen to your every thought and care, you have an entire array of people involved in your life as well. Irvin D. Yalom's *The Theory and Practice of Group Psychotherapy*, the standard text on the subject, states:

> The individual therapy format is far more insular; the group situation offers an enormous range of gratifications. To the extent that the group is a social microcosm, it contains the possibilities of satisfying virtually any social need in an individual's life.

In short, in group you meet all kinds, and this variety is enormously satisfying. A group member can be mothered by one person, intellectually challenged by another, sexually sought after by yet another—the range is endless. A great deal is going on.

What is more, most people who enter therapy have led, in Yalom's phrase, an "impoverished group history." They may have had intimate relationships, they may have won success at work, but they have not had the fulfilling experience of being part of a living, breathing group. As a result, the group they become part of in therapy is a first, which makes it correspondingly harder to leave.

Moreover, in terms of transference the group stands in for a family, replete with all the standard relationships: parents, siblings, sibling rivalries. Group therapists use this psychological fact to provide a "corrective family experience" for group members. Some groups are jointly led by a male and a female therapist in order to *encourage* the family identification. When this works the group functions as a new, improved family. Problems in the members' original families are redressed in group.

While this redoing of your family of origin is a powerful therapeutic tool, leaving a family of any sort is difficult indeed. It is made even more difficult by the fact that your fellow members have a real stake in your staying. Group cohesion and stability are essential to a group's success, and when one member leaves, the group is shaken.

One of the more vivid examples of a group collapsing when members leave is Connie's story. Connie was a senior in college when she entered a group sponsored by her school's student health center. She was having problems with her love life at the time and needed help. However, she soon discovered that in her particular group romance was the least of anyone's problems. To a person, everyone there was in trouble academically. Low self-esteem, extreme procrastination, poor grades—these were the topics of the day, session after session. Although Connie had no complaints academically, she could certainly identify with low self-esteem. But in spite of her initial willingness to join in, she soon began to find the group off-putting, "creepy" even. She did not know what to attribute these negative feelings to until she recognized that each week when the group members would arrive for their session they would find that another member was *gone*.

While client-therapist confidentiality precluded the group leaders (a man and a woman) from giving details, enough was said to indicate that each newly missing member had left school. And as Connie remembers the scene, it was almost worse not having the specifics. Members' imaginations could run wild. Had Bob or Jane or whoever been thrown out? Could he or she ever come back? The atmosphere grew increasingly grim.

The result for the group was that sessions quickly took on the tone and feel of a wake. Each week the little band of survivors would turn up, each week another of their number would be missing, each week they would mourn that member's passing—and wonder secretly who would be next. And *no one* would give voice to that sentiment. It was dreadful.

Naturally, these ongoing departures completely destroyed the group's effectiveness. "After a while you just felt like you were hanging out with this collection of losers," Connie remembers, "as if everyone in the group was *marked*." Her defense was to withdraw emotionally; *she* didn't have any of these problems. Soon after she withdrew physically as well, leaving the group. After that experience, she reports today, she would never consider going into group therapy again.

In this case, of course, termination was a sign of failure, but even when termination is a sign of success, it can be just as problematic from the group's point of view. Comparisons unavoidably arise. If you want to leave because you are better, what does this say about those you are leaving behind? It says that they are not better, that they have not reached your point. Other members may bring pressure on you to stay, not to take any action that reflects badly upon their own progress. Furthermore, in retrospect many people say they were helped most not by the therapist but by other members of the group. Naturally no one wants to lose a fellow member who is helping him with his own problems.

And finally, with group therapy you come face-to-face with a real-life example of the old saying that you cannot step in the same river twice. Leaving group is uniquely difficult in that it is uniquely final. The group flows on after you go, changing always; new members arrive, old members move on. You can never come back to the exact same group you left. Where an individual psychotherapist can offer you the reassuring thought that you can return if you need to, no group therapist can say the same. When you are leaving a group, the sense of loss is absolute.

So when and how do you leave a group? The same criteria you use for leaving individual psychotherapy apply, but with one additional caveat. People who leave prematurely—which Yalom defines as after less than twelve sessions—often feel worse than they did when they began group. Yalom advises a twelve- to twenty-four-month time period for group therapy as a general rule.

It is also widely held that your decision to leave should be discussed with the group. If *everyone* agrees that it is too soon, it may well be. In spite of all the emotional forces working against letting a member go, if it really is time for you to leave, a couple of members will be strong enough to say so.

An abrupt decision to terminate is particularly questionable. If you find yourself making sudden, out-of-the-blue announcements that you are leaving, consider two possibilities: you may be leaving too soon, or you may be leaving at the right time but without being able to say thank you or knowing how to offer a warm goodbye. When the latter is the case, how to say goodbye becomes the one final problem to work on in group.

While group therapists frown on abrupt departures, they nevertheless treat termination as a relatively brisk and informal process. Generally you will be expected to spend only a few weeks discussing your plans to leave and working through your—and the other members'—feelings about going. In group the ending is not dragged out. It makes sense that group therapists do not believe in lengthy terminations, since in group whenever one patient terminates, he does so on the time of everyone else. To focus half a year or more on one member's going could significantly distort the topics the other patients bring up. Moreover, by the time the terminating member actually left, another one would no doubt be embarking on his own six months. The group could end up spending all its time on termination alone.

For group therapy to be successful, it is essential to *like* your group. Researchers have found that patients who do not like their groups do not fare well. Also, patients popular with other members of the group have far and away the most successful outcomes. If you do not feel accepted and liked by your fellow group members, this is not the group for you. And if you feel negative about them, again, you should search for a new group.

Don't make the mistake of getting trapped in a hostile group in order to prove something to yourself—or to them. And don't try to win a group over. The group must be cohesive, and you must feel basically positive toward your group leaders, or progress will not happen. If you are not happy in your group, find another, or leave group therapy altogether.

Whether you are leaving a group or an individual therapy, you face the universal experience of loss. The challenge, as with all separations, is to move on when the time has come: to recognize that time and to act. A good termination will see you through.

WHEN YOUR THERAPIST LEAVES YOU

While any termination brings up issues of separation and loss, a termination initiated by your therapist tends to stir up issues of rejection and abandonment as well. The result can be devastating—or it can give you the extra push you need to move on.

The most benign case occurs when your therapist leaves you purely because external events dictate he must. He may be graduating from his program, changing jobs, moving away; he may even be leaving the profession. Or he may be seriously ill. Whatever the reason, while your therapy is being ended according to something other than what you want and need, still you are not being rejected or thrown out. You don't have to take it personally.

Unfortunately, even this kind of ending can be extremely painful. Jennifer discovered just how painful when she entered therapy with a man who was doing his postdoctoral work at her local university. He had helped her overcome the depression and bulimia that had long plagued her, and she treasured his presence in

164

her life. As a therapist he was supportive in approach, telling her frequently that she was a good person, an intelligent person, a person who "could handle her life if she chose to." He saw her, he said, as a woman who might stumble a lot, but who could always pick herself back up. Jennifer became powerfully attached to him. More, she viewed him with a mixture of envy and awe: slightly younger than she, he was already doing post-doctorate work at a major university. She herself had not gone to college after high school and was only now, at age thirty, working toward her degree.

She knew from the beginning that their time together would be finite. He would be finishing his program in two and a half years and planned to move at that point. While this planned separation loomed on the horizon for the entire course of her therapy, Jennifer put off thinking about it until six or seven months before the scheduled date. All along she sustained herself with fantasies that somehow "he would stay, or I would stay, or we would ride off into the sunset together." But no such last-minute reprieve was to come, and in June of their third year together, both Jennifer and her therapist graduated from their respective programs and moved away to new employment.

Many months later, Jennifer has not yet recovered. She found the termination extremely painful, and she thinks of her therapist every day. She fantasizes about him, sometimes writes him letters (which he answers), and rereads the journal she kept during their time together as a way of recapturing those days—as a way of, in her words, "holding on." There have been times since her therapy ended when she did not think she could make it without him—though the gains she made in therapy have held. Her problem now is not that she fears a relapse into depression and bulimia; it is that she misses her therapist terribly—this in spite of the fact that she and her therapist devoted a full six months to discussing her feelings about his move. Together, they discovered that her reaction was connected with her mother's death six years before. Even now she still thinks of her mother daily; she often wishes she could pick up the phone and call her. Having suffered the traumatic loss of a parent, Jennifer responded to her therapist's leaving as a kind of death. She literally mourned his loss.

Again, the issue of who leaves whom can be extremely delicate. In terms of transference, having your therapist leave you can powerfully reawaken your most profound experiences of loss. And the feelings of abandonment that all patients feel to some extent when they leave therapy become all the more intense when it is the therapist who ends things.

In Jennifer's case one wonders whether she should have been seeing this particular therapist at all, given that she knew from the outset he would be leaving. Since her mother's death had been so overwhelming, perhaps she should have chosen a therapist whose career was well established in her city. At the very least she would then have been in charge of deciding when to terminate, an arrangement that could have given her some sense of control over loss and separation, which might have helped her cope better with her mother's death.

If you know that your fundamental problems concern loss, abandonment, and death, look for a therapist you can count on to remain safely established in your hometown. Young therapists who are still completing their training are frequently forced to leave behind patients who still need them. This is a constant source of frustration to the therapists themselves, who in some cases are required by the structure of their programs to rotate among assignments. But it can be much more than frustrating to you.

While it can be difficult to lose your therapist because of a career change, relocation, or ill health, the more complex issues are raised when your therapist encourages you to leave simply because he feels it is time for you to go. Some patients take their therapist's suggestion that they terminate in stride, but many more suffer. Of the people I spoke with whose therapists had encouraged them to leave, several felt actively hurt; the rest had taken the suggestion well enough but were now in therapy with another therapist. Certainly, none of them believed—even in retrospect—that he really had been ready to terminate when his therapist said so.

Nevertheless, therapists who have researched the subject do offer case histories of patients who benefited from being pushed to terminate. Firestein describes a therapeutic situation in which a therapist-initiated termination helped: it is, paradoxically, a case in which the patient was so unnerved by the prospect of eventual termination that she could get nothing accomplished in the first place. At the outset, Charlotte entered therapy for several reasons: she very much feared sexual relations; she could not be interested in men who were interested in her; and she had trouble speaking before a group, especially when men were likely to be present.

During her opening interview, Charlotte confided she so feared being rejected by men that she often broke off her relationships for that reason alone, operating on the you-can't-fire-me-I-quit principle. This fear proved to be a major obstacle to her therapy. Her therapist was male, and, because of her defenses against growing too attached to a man, she had enormous difficulty establishing a positive therapeutic alliance with him. Instead, in her therapist's view, she defended herself against warm feelings for him by violently transforming them into their opposite. Thus, for nearly five years, Charlotte heaped "every conceivable derogation" upon her doctor in order to avoid falling dramatically in love with—or dramatically into dependence on—him.

Her therapist came to feel that Charlotte's conflicts concerning separation were at the root of her problems. She became enraged by any weekend separation from her current boyfriend, and she had trouble handling her therapist's summer vacations as well. Finally, during the fifth year of her analysis, he proposed setting a definite termination date—well into the future—as a way of allaying her anxiety over losing him. His reasoning was that if Charlotte knew precisely when her analysis was going to end, she would be able to stop worrying that some day her therapy *might* end. A *fait accompli*, he felt, would be easier for her to deal with than a terrifying possibility.

He was right. When he introduced the idea of fixing a termination date as a means of improving their therapeutic relationship, Charlotte responded well. In fact, she was actually pleased something was being done to move her therapy forward. She herself set the time, choosing a date one year hence—an act which gave her a crucial sense of control—and she was able to work productively with her therapist from that point on.

Charlotte's case is evidence that there are times when having your therapist initiate your termination can be good for you. However, Charlotte was not simply ushered out. Her therapist brought up the topic of termination as a way of helping her therapy, not sum-

marily ending it, and Charlotte herself chose the date.
Clearly, for a therapist-initiated termination to work,
the patient eventually has to become *actively involved*
in the decision.

When a patient does not become actively involved,
things do not go quite so well, even if the therapist is
absolutely right in encouraging his patient to leave.
Wallerstein describes the case of "Phobic Woman," so
named because she was terrified of being left alone—to
the point that her husband could not even leave the
house for a haircut. Haircuts had to come to him; he
paid his barber to drive to their home, comb and scis-
sors in hand. From Phobic Woman's perspective therapy offered the ultimate opportunity for total
dependence, for being taken care of by father (who was
in fact paying for the treatment), mother, and husband
in one. Phobic Woman might well have stayed in analysis forever if her analyst had allowed it. But he did not.
After four years of analysis Phobic Woman had made
tremendous progress; her life had taken on the rhythms
and cycles of normalcy. She could now spend time
away from her husband, who was able to return to
school, graduate, and go on to graduate studies. She
herself finished college, and found the confidence to
have a child, then to become pregnant with a second.
At this point, her therapist moved to bring her analysis
to an end.

Though termination was very much against Phobic
Woman's wishes, inevitably the end arrived. And two
years later a follow-up session revealed that her improvements had held up overall though she was somewhat more symptomatic than when she had left therapy.
Nonetheless, she still did not feel she had been ready to
terminate when she did—though on the other hand she
did not long to return to her therapist. She thought she

might seek help elsewhere, possibly in the form of a briefer therapy. Twenty years later she herself had become a therapist.

Clearly, Phobic Woman continued to have regrets. She did not want to leave therapy when she did, and she does not seem ever to have completely made peace with the fact that her therapy ended against her wishes. Nevertheless, it is not a good thing for a grown woman to live out her life as a psychological child, and her therapist had good reason for what he did. It is possible he had taken her as far as he could in the direction of adulthood. In her words, during the course of therapy her father and her doctor had "grown smaller and smaller," while she and her husband had "grown bigger and bigger." Her therapist, in pushing for termination, was insisting that his patient take this process to its logical end, that she grow up all the way.

In short, on a transference level, what her therapist did amounted to pushing his patient out of the nest. Very probably, he was right to do so—and while Phobic Woman was not happy about it, she did do well outside therapy. All of which means that a therapist *can* end your therapy for your own good, even when you are dead set against it. While you may never come to see things his way, if your life moves forward after therapy ends, you can tell yourself that at least his intentions were good.

On the other hand, there are clearly cases when a therapist has made the wrong decision concerning his patient's readiness to end therapy. Originally Sharon began seeing a therapist at a county health clinic because of problems in her long-term relationship with Pauline, her lover. She was also finding it hard living near her East Coast family again after many years away. But when her therapy ended against her wishes, and then a *second* therapy ended the same way, her problem became termination itself. Embarking on her third therapy, what she most needed help dealing with was the premature and involuntary endings of the previous two.

Sharon's first involuntary termination occurred after she and Pauline both entered individual therapy with two separate therapists. Sharon preferred this arrangement; she says she chose individual therapy in part because "I wanted something of my own." But soon Pauline's therapist strongly recommended that the two women see her together for couples counseling. Though Sharon did not want to do this, everyone around her was in favor of it; even her own therapist told her she should move on to couples counseling with Pauline's therapist. Unfortunately, to have her therapist urge her to move on to another therapist *felt*, to Sharon, like a forced termination. Whether it genuinely *was* forced— whether her therapist would have kept Sharon as a patient if she had insisted—we can't know. But the truth is, having a therapist tell her to move on created a catch-22. Once Sharon had been put in the position of having to try to talk her therapist into remaining her therapist, she had already "lost." Even if Sharon's first therapist had agreed to stay on the case, Sharon was simply not going to be able to build a warm and trusting alliance with someone who was seeing her expressly against her better judgment. In effect, Sharon was forced out the moment her therapist strongly urged her to leave. In acquiescing to the wishes of everyone around her, she was simply bowing to reality.

Sharon's second therapy ended even more badly. When, after many months of joint sessions with Sharon, Pauline decided to end their relationship, she also ended their couples counseling. She would no longer be going to sessions with Sharon. This was understandable, but to Sharon's great dismay, abruptly her own therapy was over as well. Without warning, and certainly without any formal termination period, Pauline's therapist simply ended Sharon's therapy during her last joint session with Pauline. Since she had seen Pauline first, Sharon's soon-to-be-ex-therapist now said, she could not continue to see Sharon alone. She could see only Pauline alone. Worse, this surprise final session came at a time when the therapist had been actively praising Sharon for learning to trust her. Recently Sharon had found herself able to call the therapist for help if she needed attention between sessions, which, in her therapist's view, signaled a breakthrough in Sharon's capacity to depend on others.

Sharon was infuriated by her therapist's decision: "One week she was praising my 'dependence'; the next week she was saying, 'Depend on somebody else.'" She was also devastated by the double loss: lover and therapist both gone in one blow. Even so, for all her pain and anger, Sharon had little choice but to acquiesce. It wasn't up to her, and arguing about it wasn't going to change things. Besides, she had no desire to try to talk her way back into her own therapy. As she put it, "If that was the way she felt, then to hell with her."

So Sharon moved on to a third therapist. By now her problem was not her relationship with Pauline, but her relationship with Pauline's therapist. She needed help getting over her anger at having been thrown out of therapy by someone she needed. Unfortunately, the third therapy proved to be the most painful of all. Sharon fell deeply in love with her new therapist, who ultimately ended up leaving the profession, abandoning Sharon to the fates. After three therapies Sharon found herself in the ironic position of having acquired an entirely new problem she needed help with: termination.

Sharon's story is a disturbing one. Certainly the forced termination by the couples therapist was bad for her. In terms of transference, it can only wreak havoc on an already hurting patient to lose both lover *and* therapist at once. One wonders what effect this forced termination had on the course of her third and very painful therapy. Would Sharon have fallen so hopelessly in love with this therapist if she had not been pushed away by the preceding one?

Having been pushed out of therapy twice probably played a role in setting up her final therapist as an elusive—and hence desirable—figure. For Sharon, therapist-initiated terminations indeed seem to have proved destructive.

Sharon's therapists believed they were acting in her best interest. Simple misjudgments were involved. The worst-case scenario happens when a therapist pushes his patient out of therapy for emotional reasons entirely his own. When the therapist's countertransference motivates his desire that his patient leave, the results can be devastating.

Rebecca is one patient who experienced a "countertransference termination." Nearly twenty years ago, when she became pregnant out of wedlock at the age of seventeen, her parents committed her to a mental hospital—a response which, while unthinkable today, was possible at that time in the conservative Midwestern community where Rebecca and her parents lived.

Her psychotherapy there was not helpful, and ultimately her therapist himself confessed the reason why: he was physically attracted to his young, pregnant patient, he said. Because of this attraction, he was terminating her therapy.

This was a countertransference termination: a termination forced by the therapist because of his own unmanageable—and in this case inappropriate —reactions to his patient. And while he was right to end Rebecca's treatment, the effect on her seems to have been destructive. Already in shock over being pregnant and confined to a mental institution, Rebecca now had to deal with the implications of an illicit desire on the part of her male therapist. Twenty years later, she is still seeking, in essence, the perfect therapist. She has been in therapy most of the time since that episode, with little improvement to show for it. It seems quite possible that this early countertransference termination was sufficiently traumatic to set her on a course of therapy "rebounds": one unsatisfactory and disturbing therapy set her up for the next, and so on. Rebecca may be a woman who has spent half a lifetime trying to rewrite one early therapy and its termination.

While relatively few patients face this situation, one final, and unique, category of involuntary termination is the sudden and shattering loss of a therapist to suicide. Although therapists as a group are probably no more personally troubled than any other professionals, they do face the emotional challenge of listening to other people's problems day in and day out. According to the well-established psychological concept of "mood contagion," moods—especially bad moods—are contagious, which means that a daily communion with other people's dark feelings is bound to take its toll. In short, for therapists depression would seem to be a genuine occupational hazard.

When a patient loses a therapist to suicide, the results are calamitous. Karen's story is among the most traumatic. She had been seeing her therapist for *fifteen years* when he killed himself. His suicide alone would have been enough to shock her deeply, but she subsequently learned that he had killed himself because he was being sued by several clients. He had been taking drugs and engaging in orgies with some of his patients, all of them young males. A married man and a father, he could not face the public scandal that was about to erupt.

Karen felt utter rage, to the point of wishing to file her own suit against his estate. She had loved and trusted this man for fifteen years. Worse, she had gone to him with her own heterosexual love-life problems— none of which had ever appreciably improved. After a brief, disastrous marriage in her early twenties she had remained alone, much against her wishes. "Over the years I kept asking him," she recalls now, " 'Aren't I missing something? Isn't something wrong?' And he kept saying, 'No, there's nothing wrong with you. It's hard to meet people. The right one will come along.' Now I feel I wasted fifteen years."

To feel that you have wasted so much time because of your psychiatrist's personal pathology is devastating. Perhaps Karen should have realized she was getting nowhere a dozen years ago and switched therapists, but in fact her therapist *was* helping her significantly in the career realm. Moreover, he had been her mentor when she studied psychology in graduate school. He was a powerfully established authority figure in her life; he was right about most issues; and she simply took it on faith he must be right about love, too. It *is* hard to meet men; there *are* a lot of confirmed bachelors out there. The sentiments he was expressing jibed with her own perceptions and with those of her friends. These feelings combined to keep her in therapy with a deeply disturbed professional.

As she struggled to make sense of her therapist's suicide, Karen's whole worldview was thrown into chaos. Had he been good for her? Had he been bad for her? How much of both? Why hadn't she known? How much else didn't she know about the people she trusted? She is now confronted by so many questions and doubts that she may never truly be able to put his death to rest. And although a new therapist might be able to help, Karen is in no mood to trust a new therapist— and probably in no condition to choose the one she needs.

The good news is that with the help of the right therapist you *can* put such a loss to rest. Larry is a former patient who was able successfully to work through his therapist's suicide with the help of a second therapist. A graduate student in his early twenties, Larry had been in therapy for two years when his therapist committed suicide. He had the bad luck to arrive at his therapist's office for an appointment at the very moment police were discovering his therapist's body at home. When Larry called his therapist's apartment to find out whether there had been some snag, an unknown man answered curtly with a demand that Larry identify himself. Larry did, and then asked to whom he was speaking. The answer, Larry recalls, "was like something out of a Sherlock Holmes novel: 'I am Detective Sergeant McGinty and Dr. Montague is dead!' "

The policeman then insisted that Larry come to his therapist's apartment, and when he arrived he was greeted by the sight of his therapist's dead body lying crumpled on the floor, beneath a sheet. The police clearly suspected Larry of being involved in what they thought was a murder, and he was made to submit to questioning in his dead therapist's kitchen.

Though Larry was quickly cleared of suspicion (the death was in fact a suicide), he felt terrible about having been oblivious to his therapist's suffering. In what turned out to be their final session together, Larry had made a comment that had seemed to upset his therapist, who had said, "Oh, so if it works out I'll get the credit for it, and if it doesn't you'll blame me." The remark had been disturbing at the time, since Larry had not meant his comment to be taken that way. But after the death this exchange loomed large and Larry felt he had added immeasurably to his therapist's suffering during his last days on earth.

Having been literally under suspicion of murder did not help matters. Transference does not stop on a dime just because the person you've been transferring *to* is suddenly deceased. And, finally, when Larry walked into his therapist's apartment, he was symbolically walking into a final session. The emotional ramifications were overwhelming.

Larry also felt profoundly abandoned. Abandonment had been one of his issues since the age of four, when he was taken to the hospital and left there for major surgery. At that time (the 1940s) parents were allowed to visit their hospitalized children only twice a week. A small boy, he had had to survive surgery and a painful convalescence alone in the hospital for ten days. The loss of his therapist now brought on a sweeping sense of *déjà vu:* for a second time he was left behind by a person he depended on.

It was a terrible passage in his life. But Larry, unlike Karen, found real help from another therapist—this time a woman, who helped him enormously with his sense of guilt. Fortunately he had, as he puts it, a strong grip on reality. With a new, emotionally healthy therapist to validate his perceptions, he was able to move his departed therapist out of transference and back to real life. He came to realize that his therapist was *trained* not to reveal himself; Larry could not have known how unhappy he was. He was not responsible. Further, he *believed* he was not responsible. Even so, today, twenty years later, his therapist's suicide remains a vivid memory for Larry.

For any patient who faces this tragedy, a therapist's suicide leaves him not just bereaved, abandoned, guilt-ridden, and traumatized, but bereft of meaning. And meaning is essential to well-being. If you can't *know* what has happened in your life, if you can't feel that things add up, you are on precarious footing—which is precisely the state of affairs that brought you to therapy in the first place.

A termination through suicide is, of course, extremely rare. Its hallmark is the total shock and surprise that accompany any sudden death of a parent, mate, or friend, which is part of what makes it such a destructive way to end psychotherapeutic treatment. To be constructive, the process of termination *must* allow the patient ample time to prepare and come to grips with the impending separation.

With this in mind, the first thing to do when your therapist brings up termination before you feel ready is not to bolt, but to discuss the situation thoroughly. Why is he pushing you to leave? What does he think you—or your therapy—will gain from setting a date? He may believe that setting a final date will actually improve your therapy in the time remaining, and subsequent sessions may prove him to be right. A formal termination is *part* of therapy, so if you postpone it indefinitely you are cheating yourself out of one phase of what you are there for. Your therapist may indeed be doing this for your own good, and discussing his reasons with him may convince you that this is so.

The days of talking the proposed termination through should also help you shake the feeling of being passively moved to and fro by an all-powerful therapist. When you and your therapist discuss your termination at length, you begin, through simple talk, to shape its reality—to claim the action for yourself even though your therapist has set things in motion. Your interpretation of events shifts: you begin to see that you are not being rejected, but are participating in an important decision concerning your life. Setting the date yourself is especially helpful in this process. When you choose the precise day of your final session, you take action—even if it is action taken under protest. Acting is always more satisfying than simply being moved along by the course of events; certainly the capacity to take action is one of the universal goals of successful therapy.

This, of course, happens in the best of all possible worlds. The trouble comes when you absolutely are not ready to leave, but the therapy is terminated nonetheless, often for reasons that have nothing to do with you. When this occurs, you may suffer the entire spectrum of unhappy emotions: anger, sadness, feelings of rejection and abandonment, rage. And while strong emotion fades in time, what does not fade is the profound sense of *confusion* a forced termination tends to produce. You just don't know, and you may never know, *why.*

To recover from a forced termination, you have to recover your own sense of what is true and what is not. And very likely, you will need help to do so. If a therapist cuts your therapy off for irrational reasons of his own, it is best not to try to handle it by yourself. You should probably not tackle it alone even if you believe your therapist has acted purely out of positive motives. What you have undergone, apart from a powerful emotional experience, is an equally powerful assault on your sense of reality. More specifically, you have suffered an attack on your sense of *social reality*, of what was going on between the two of you in that office. And social reality, in order to *feel* like reality, cannot exist simply in your own head. If you and you alone say to yourself, "It's not me, it's my therapist," you will not be sufficiently convinced. A perception that *you alone hold* is going to feel tenuous at best—especially since you may have gone into therapy in the first place already doubting your perceptions. When it comes to social reality we all need others to validate our perceptions. This is exactly as it should be; we could have no social cohesion whatsoever if everyone simply assumed that whatever fleeting thoughts crossed his mind concerning others were absolutely and unquestionably true. Social reality rides on consensus.

If you are the victim of a forced termination, it is essential to find trusted family, friends, or lovers to help you establish (or reestablish) your own vision of reality. And in those cases where friends and family are not going to be enough, the only possible course may be Larry's: to seek therapy for leaving therapy.

The danger in these cases is therapy on the rebound. Like love on the rebound, a new therapeutic relationship that begins in the wake of an earlier, disastrous therapeutic relationship is heavily loaded from the beginning. Not only do you have all the normal transference issues to cope with; you have transference issues specifically concerning therapy and therapists as well. A vicious cycle can commence; a patient can move from therapist to therapist for years, acting out his termination fears over and over again.

When going into therapy to get over therapy, you should make your situation known at the outset. Very possibly you should opt for brief therapy at this point: the overt time restrictions could be useful in warding off the overattachment that can develop when you're hurting from a "rejection" by a previous therapist.

Most good therapists have had the experience of helping patients work through conflicts concerning earlier therapies—and a good therapist will make his ability to help with this clear early on. From there therapy for leaving therapy can turn into therapy for all the right reasons, therapy to restore your right to a share in life.

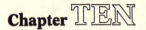

POWER STRUGGLES

Eventually most therapists will do their best to see you through termination. However, there *are* some therapists who will not let go. And when you are in treatment with a therapist who is determined to hold on, you face a struggle.

Often, this struggle comes to be about power, as simple disagreement escalates to outright conflict. A therapist who does not want to let go will be tempted to employ subtle (and sometimes not-so-subtle) tactics to hold you in place, and in some cases, he will yield to temptation. When this happens your therapist is no longer trying to *persuade* you to stay but to *make* you stay.

Melissa can attest to the trauma that results from an out-and-out power struggle with a therapist. Long before her stormy departure she knew her doctor was preoccupied with power: during sessions he routinely practiced the tactics of intimidation, once even exploding in rage when Melissa, who had been complaining about the cost of therapy, bought a new car. Cowed by him, Melissa found herself unable to break free for many months even though she very much wanted to do

182

so. She assumed—rightly, as it turned out—that the very topic of termination would set off a struggle.

Finally, after a trip to Europe had given her some distance from the situation, she returned to therapy and informed her therapist that she was terminating. As she feared, he did not react well. "You can't just walk in here and quit," he said firmly, as if she were violating the bylaws of therapy. Then he delivered what amounted to a therapeutic rabbit punch: he told her she needed to explore why she wanted to leave therapy; she was doing the same thing with him, he said, that she did with men. To Melissa, the implication was clear: she was a failure in love and a failure in therapy, too.

She was far too devastated by this assessment of her character to leave therapy. The topic of termination now died away. Though her therapist had agreed to a formal termination that was to last, he said, from three to five sessions, the subject did not come up again. He did not raise it, and Melissa found herself too intimidated to bring it up herself. "I realize now," she says, "that I was afraid he was going to pull more of this logic about my love life if I mentioned leaving again, and I just couldn't take it."

After this she spent many months wanting to leave, but feeling unable to summon the strength: therapy, for her, had become a contest of wills. Finally, after a happy visit from the man with whom she had been in love for five years (the two of them lived in different cities), she drew up a list of resolutions for a stronger, healthier life. Among them was leaving therapy.

Fearing another power struggle with her therapist, this time she did not confront him face-to-face. Instead she called his service and canceled her next appointment. She had decided simply to "drop out."

Her therapist, however, was far from willing to let

her go so easily. He promptly called her at home to reschedule the missed appointment and when he discovered she had no intention of rescheduling said angrily, "You absolutely cannot do this. This is a decision two people make. You are making a big mistake, and you're going to wipe out everything you've gained."

Finally, Melissa gave way, more distraught now over therapy itself than she had ever been about the problems she had come to therapy to solve. Worn down, she agreed to return for another session. But when her friends (one of whom was himself a therapist) universally advised her not to return she canceled this appointment as well. Her therapist called her again—at work this time—shouting furiously at her over the phone. "He just kept saying, 'You can't leave,' over and over again," Melissa recalls.

Obviously, this is an extreme case, as the therapist who ultimately helped Melissa find her way out of this devastating situation made clear. Her new therapist did not mince words, and he made no effort to "psychologize" Melissa's role in the struggle; what Melissa was dealing with, he said, was highly unprofessional behavior, pure and simple. There was absolutely no reason for her to be plunged into self-doubt over leaving therapy with a bad therapist.

Fortunately, few patients will be faced with the challenge of ending treatment with a therapist who is both preoccupied with power and just plain unprofessional —but it does happen. If you do find yourself in this situation a good therapist can be enormously helpful. What you need is someone to validate your perceptions, and having a good therapist to back you up is probably the best approach. While your friends and family will obviously take your side, a part of you is going to wonder whether they are defending you simply because they are friends and family. When another therapist tells you that you are facing unprofessional behavior, you are more likely to be convinced. Certainly Melissa found her new therapist's support indispensable in shaking off the fear and worry her former therapist had produced. Moreover, her new therapist approached the entire situation as a temporary crisis. He did not advise Melissa to enter long-term therapy with him, though she knew she was welcome to do so if she wished.

As destructive as Melissa's situation was, it does have the virtue of being clear-cut. The appropriate response was clear-cut as well: Melissa needed to leave this therapist at once, without agreeing to a termination process. The more common problem with power struggles in therapy is that typically they are very subtle—and they can happen even with a therapist who has been excellent in all other respects. In therapy, normally any struggle for power will take place at the level of symbolic gesture, ambiguous comment, veiled threat—tactics that can be unconsciously deployed by an otherwise professional and caring therapist. It can be very difficult to know whether you and your therapist are, in fact, doing "battle," in any sense of the word. And since it is difficult to know what is actually going on, it is correspondingly difficult to know how to respond.

Part of what makes a power struggle so hard to detect is the fact that a good therapist can sometimes do bad therapy. Accepting the imperfect nature of human relationships is particularly hard when it comes to therapists because they occupy such an idealized position, both in the patient's mind and in the culture at large. Transgressions you might readily forgive a friend may be deeply disturbing when coming from a therapist.

Ironically, in one respect trying to leave therapy against your therapist's will is very much like having your therapist leave you against *your* will: confusion reigns in both situations as you try to understand exactly what is happening to you, and why. Trying to decide whether you are, in fact, involved in a power struggle is a formidable task, made all the more difficult because therapists typically do not own up to their part in such a struggle. A therapist who is trying to coerce his patient into staying in therapy simply is not going to believe that the term *coerce* applies. Most probably, he will think he is doing whatever he is doing for your own good. He is certainly not likely to perceive the tactics he is employing as *tactics*.

When you see your therapy as having become coercive, while your therapist sees nothing of the sort, you face the problem of social reality. Whose perception is accurate? Therapists have little power to alter your sense of *physical* reality, but when you get to *social* reality your therapist's power takes over. Here is a "relationship," there is an "affair": the *felt* difference between these two realities depends partly on how you interpret the gestures and behaviors taking place between you and your lover. If your therapist sees your latest involvement as a mere fling, while you see it as Love at Last, you are probably going to wonder. By the same token, if you see a power struggle where your therapist sees business as usual, you are going to feel less than fully convinced that you are right. And since power struggles within therapy characteristically take place indirectly, by means of subtle acts and statements, believing your own eyes and ears can be hard.

Furthermore, if your therapist has done his job well, he has convinced you that your own eyes and ears have not always been trustworthy in the past. A good therapist will encourage you to take responsibility for your life, to understand your own role in creating or maintaining your problems and to see what you have been doing wrong that you didn't know you were doing wrong.

Unfortunately, when it comes to leaving therapy aginst your therapist's wishes, this newfound habit of questioning your motives can steer you astray. In essence, when you take responsibility for the past you rewrite history; you decide that what you thought was true actually was not. You think of yourself as having been *mistaken.* So who is to say that you aren't mistaken now, that you aren't choosing to leave therapy for wrong motives you aren't even aware of?

Laurie plunged into this form of self-doubt when she tried to end her therapy. At the start, she had gone into therapy ready—even eager—to take responsibility for the shambles her love life had become. After ending an engagement to a good man who had loved and stood by her for two years, she had met and fallen for a series of angry men who pursued her ardently, then violently withdrew from her life the moment they had won her. She wanted to know why. What was she doing wrong?

Therapy gave her the answer. Over the next months in treatment she discovered that she had been trying to work out a career trauma in the dating realm. Just after breaking off with her fiancé, she had lost her job to a hostile corporate takeover, and she had been courting loss—romantic loss—ever since. Hers was a classic effort to rewrite history on a symbolic level. She would pitch herself into an impossible situation, then try to make it come out differently—this time. Moreover, by "displacing" her career troubles to the romantic realm, she protected herself from the pain of the original loss. For Laurie it was actually less frightening, at an unconscious level, to lose boyfriends than to lose jobs. Her pattern of brief and stormy relationships was both a *symptom* of the trauma she had suffered and a *defense* against it. As she came to see her pattern of behavior clearly, her relationship with Jay, a man she had begun seeing shortly after she entered therapy, took root. The cycle was broken.

In short, her therapy was a success by her own lights. But as she discovered when she raised the possibility of leaving, her therapist did not share her pride in a therapy well done. In his view, it was clear, her new happiness in life did not necessarily mean she was *better*. "My therapist never seemed really to believe in my relationship with Jay," Laurie recalls now. "He always gave me the feeling that, while my *life* had changed, *I* hadn't." Laurie found his apparent doubt unnerving. Perhaps she *was* self-destructive, she thought; perhaps she would do something to damage this relationship, too, the way she had with her former fiancé. In spite of her happiness with Jay, maybe the old patterns were still there. Her therapist seemed to support this view. Though he seldom made outright analyses, when he did he typically remarked upon her "fear of dependence," which he clearly saw as a threat to her life with Jay.

Mired in confusion, Laurie watched herself back away from the idea of leaving. Today, she recalls the crucial exchange that transformed her desire to leave into a renewed pledge to stay: "When I first went into therapy my therapist asked me what my goals were," she says. "I said my goal was to straighten out my love life. Then, when my love life *was* straightened out and I said I was ready to leave, he asked me again what my goals were now. Somehow, just the fact that he was asking the question made me feel that I had to *have* goals—I couldn't just say I didn't have any more goals in life. So I said my new goal was not to mess things up with Jay. And once I had formulated a new goal, I had given myself a reason to stay in therapy."

Whatever her therapist's conscious—or unconscious—motivations here, in terms of power he had made a strategic move. By directing the discussion away from termination and to the issue of goals, he maneuvered Laurie into a position where she *herself* came up with the reason to stay, with only the subtlest of nudging from him. Essentially, her therapist was using the power of agenda-setting; he was defining the terms of discussion. When the terms ceased to be those of termination and became those of goal-setting, Laurie was trapped by her own logic. She had come to therapy specifically to achieve relationship goals; if she still had relationship goals she should still be in therapy.

Seven months passed and Laurie's new goal not to "mess things up" with Jay had clearly been met. They were now happily engaged and looking forward to their wedding. But again, when she raised the issue of termination, her therapist asked what her goals were. Again she found herself just pressured enough by the question that she felt she somehow had to *produce* goals. "I think I felt like he knew something I didn't," she says today, "as if by asking me what my goals were, he was hinting that there was something I needed to be working on to make sure things would be okay between Jay and me." Her new goal became not to do anything to "mess up" her marriage.

Seven months later she and Jay were happily married and Laurie was feeling extremely restless in therapy. "Basically I had been wanting out for over a year at this point," she recalls, "but my therapist was so unencouraging about the prospect that I just couldn't trust myself. I had blown a good relationship once before, I kept thinking, and maybe I would do it again. Even though everything was going great between Jay and me, I just felt so confused."

Finally, Laurie made a solid decision to leave and firmly announced her intentions to her therapist. "I must have really given him the idea I wasn't about to set any new goals," she says now, "because this time he just seemed to know I meant business." Much to her relief, her therapist now agreed to her leaving, but he advised a three- to six-month termination period. Although she felt frustrated by this new delay, she still harbored just enough doubt to think she had better take her therapist's advice. She consented and dutifully continued to appear for therapy twice a week over the next half year. "I just wanted to do everything *right*," she says.

And she wanted to be rewarded for doing so. "By the end of those five months I really wanted my therapist's blessing," she recalls. "I'd been coming to him for almost two years, during which time I had completely turned my love life around—and changed a lot of my ways of dealing with the rest of my life, too. I wanted my therapist to say I was *well*."

But her therapist remained silent on this issue, and to Laurie the covert message seemed to be that she was making a mistake in leaving therapy. This suspicion so preyed on her mind that finally she worked up the nerve to ask him outright if he thought she was ready to leave. And, after all these months of sidestepping the issue, his answer was a simple no. Her wish to leave therapy, he said, indicated difficulty committing to "open-ended relationships." When Laurie asked what an open-ended relationship was, his reply brought her up short. An open-ended relationship, he explained, was one in which you did not know the outcome—"like marriage," he said, "*or therapy.*"

Laurie took this comparison to be the veiled threat that it was. If marriage and therapy were the same kind of relationship, as her therapist seemed to imply, then you left therapy at your peril. If she had trouble committing to therapy—and clearly she did, since she was trying to leave—then she would have trouble committing to marriage. Leave therapy, and she might leave her marriage, too.

Laurie and her therapist were involved in a classic power struggle, however subtle and unacknowledged. She wanted to go; he wanted her to stay, and he was using her willingness to accept responsibility for her life to persuade her. Yet he never tried *overtly* to hold her in therapy against her will. He was at all times caring and supportive, and his efforts to persuade her to stay took place entirely on the level of suggestion. Laurie's struggle to end therapy was very different from Melissa's. Paradoxically, because Laurie's therapist was so concerned about her, and because she liked him, her termination was made all the more difficult.

The moral is, you cannot rule out the possibility of a power struggle simply because you like your therapist. Nor should you ignore subtle signs and signals that may indicate that your therapist is trying to impede your progress toward termination. Overt threats, even if not consciously intended as threats, are, of course, the most obvious signal. More difficult to discern are statements or attitudes from your therapist that upset you but that may or may not be threats. Probably the most common of these is simple vagueness: when you bring up termination your therapist appears not to approve of the idea, but refuses to explain why. Instead, perhaps he will say only that you are "not ready." Naturally, this doesn't tell you much—but further explanation is rarely forthcoming.

For example, one therapist, pressed for elaboration, volunteered that therapy has a beginning, a middle, and an end, and that his patient was "somewhere in the

middle." Another, whose client was leaving therapy because her father refused to continue footing the $400
weekly bill, told her that analysis lasts from four to
eight years, depending upon the person. When the patient asked what sort of person she was, he answered
that she was "more the eight-year type." Such re-
sponses are unnerving because you wonder what it is
your therapist is *not* saying. And they can have the effect of convincing you to stay in spite of your desire to
go. When this is the case, you are justified in suspecting
at least a low-level power struggle.

Another common tactic therapists use is avoidance,
or simply sidestepping the issue of termination. You
bring it up, your therapist responds blandly, and then
it is on to other business. Maybe you bring it up again,
and your therapist again responds with only the mildest flicker of interest before moving on to other things.
You come to therapy planning to talk about termination; you leave having spent the hour discussing your
mother. When your desire to terminate gets derailed in
this fashion—especially when it happens repeatedly—
you should suspect that you and your therapist are
working at odds.

A much more nebulous sign of struggle is your therapist's tendency to overanalyze your life. Think of Steve.
His therapist tried to hold him in therapy by refusing
to accept Steve's parting gift until Steve had analyzed
why he had given it. Steve's therapist was transforming
an action (drawing a cartoon for his therapist) into a
symptom (Why a cartoon? Why this particular cartoon?). This is a relatively clear-cut case of overanalyzing a patient; *whatever* Steve meant by giving his
therapist a gift, this was no longer an appropriate topic
of discussion. Steve was leaving, and his gift should
have been accepted as simply a gift.

Deciding whether your therapist is overanalyzing

you is not easy. After all, analysis is his job; that's what you are in therapy for. The main time to concern yourself with the possibility of overanalysis is when your therapist analyzes not just your life in general, but your desire to leave therapy in particular. Laurie's therapist took this tack when he construed her decision to terminate as a symptom of her inability to keep commitments even though, in fact, her therapy had helped her *make* a commitment to marriage. *This* is a case of overanalysis.

Often, a therapist who interprets your desire to leave as typical of some larger problem you are having in life may be guilty of overanalysis. Frequently, for instance, a therapist will suggest in so many words that your wish to leave betrays a certain cowardice. "If you're leaving now," the reasoning goes, "just when we're getting somewhere, then you are afraid to face your real problems." This argument carries weight because very often therapy does become more productive during termination—which can make you suspect you might be jumping ship just as therapy is getting "deep."

Alternatively, a therapist may subtly accuse you of not trusting him or her—thus responding to the potential criticism your leaving implies. If, in fact, you *aren't* feeling much trust in your therapist at the moment, this feeling then becomes grist for the mill; you and your therapist begin to "work on" your lack of trust. But if you believe that your leaving has nothing to do with trust one way or the other, you can easily get locked into trying to prove it. The upshot is your staying in therapy longer than you wish.

Errors or so-called Freudian slips can also be significant signals of a power struggle, just as much so for the therapist as for the patient. Remember Bill, whose therapist mistakenly believed he had published his book with a "small Southern press." You are justified in assuming that this kind of mistake is more than a lapse. It is a way of maintaining superiority—and quite possibly of holding a patient in therapy. Just prior to this exchange, Bill had several times brought up his desire to end therapy, which his therapist had steadfastly argued against. Making Bill feel "small" may have been a way of keeping him in therapy.

Finally, frequent repetition can be a sign of a subtle power struggle. Repeated forgetting of information that is important to you, repeated slips of the tongue, and repeated failures to respond to a subject you have raised are all clues that something more than mere forgetfulness is involved; your therapist may be trying to keep the upper hand.

Beyond these tangible, and discrete, signs of trouble, look for an overall *pattern* of subtle bids for control. Ginny, a fiction writer who lived alone, went into therapy after a long, solitary depression. Her suffering was so intense that she was experiencing psychic blackouts. Moments of time escaped her; driving down the street she would suddenly become aware that she was several blocks away from where she had been the last time she had had any sense of time and place—and she could call up no memory of how she had gotten there. It was terrifying.

A friend recommended a therapist to Ginny, whom she began seeing once a week. Although her blackouts subsided in time, she always felt uneasy about her therapist, who seemed to want exclusive access to her time and attention. He pressed constantly for an increase in the number of sessions per week, and he seemed almost to compete with the men in her life for her affection and respect. Invariably, he reacted with skepticism to any new man she met, and though he was usually on the mark—most of the men she came across were not good candidates for a happy relationship—his consistent negativity troubled her. In session, none of her suitors had a chance. Her therapist seemed to be setting himself up as her one and only.

Even more unsettling to Ginny was his reaction to her writing. At thirty she was publishing her second novel and was an established free-lance journalist. She was quite successful for her age, but her therapist seemed often to call the reality of her accomplishments into question. Clearly he had never read her work, and whenever the subject came up he questioned her in a manner that betrayed a certain incredulity. "*Where* did you say you published your novel?" he would ask, never seeming to remember he had asked the same question the session before. "I always got the feeling he didn't really believe I had published any novels," Ginny recalls. "It seemed to me as if he was fishing for a confession—as if once I was healthy again I would let go of this delusional fantasy that I was a writer."

This, together with his dismissal of the men she saw, slowly made Ginny feel that her therapist wanted her existence all to himself—that he wanted *control*. In session, the reality of her life outside therapy turned shadowy. Her novels, her men—neither were a strong presence when she sat face-to-face with her therapist.

When she detected a consistent pattern of repetition and negativity, her trust faded and she realized she could make no further progress, let alone work toward a successsful termination. She quit therapy abruptly, sending her therapist a letter announcing her departure. Two days later he took the unprecedented action of calling her at home. He was concerned by her decision, he said, because if Ginny left treatment now she faced "a complete breakdown."

This warning, however well intentioned, amounted to nothing less than an out-and-out threat. It confirmed Ginny's perception that her therapist meant to hold on to her, that, in fact, she *was* involved with someone who insisted on having the upper hand. While she was shocked and disturbed by his dark prediction for her future without him—which proved to be unfounded—a part of her was glad he had made the call. By stepping so far over the line her therapist dispelled Ginny's lingering doubts as to whether she had been right to leave therapy.

Overall, in trying to decide whether or not you are involved in a power struggle of whatever dimension, you should look for even the subtlest signs that your therapist is trying to hold you in a dependent role. After all, the proper goal of therapy is to help you achieve *independence.* If your therapist ever so slightly puts down your accomplishments, or ever so slightly but consistently casts doubt on all of your major relationships, these innuendoes will tend to make you feel that you can't go it alone—that now is not the time to leave.

Once you have decided that all is not well between you and your therapist, your first move is to discuss this with him directly. Although you can, like Ginny, simply up and quit, an abrupt ending can leave you with a great deal of unfinished business. The odds are that your therapist means well, and very likely you *believe* he means well in spite of your present suspicions. Give him the benefit of the doubt. Discuss your misgivings directly, and give him a chance to explain himself. If he clearly believes that he is acting in your best interests, you may still have to leave against his wishes, but at least you will not have to suffer the trauma of suddenly feeling that you have been deluded or mistreated for the entire course of your therapy.

Furthermore, given the nature of the transference that leads you to associate your therapist with your parents, an abrupt break-off can actually be destructive. Coming to terms with your parents is essential to a reasonably free and strong adult life; by the same token, making peace with your therapist is also wise. You want to *conclude* therapy, not just escape. Moreover, you want to finish therapy by restoring your therapist to normalcy, so that he is neither hero nor villain.

Basically, the only way to confront a power struggle is to raise the issue openly in session. Bill did this, in part, through a symbolic gesture. The week after the "small Southern press" exchange, Bill went to his session and did not lie down on the couch as usual. Instead he sat in a chair directly in front of his therapist and looked him in the eye. In essence, he refused—consciously—to play the patient. His therapist observed, "You've chosen to sit in the chair today."

Be prepared for this mode of response when you raise the subject of power struggles with your own therapist. Within the profession it is known as "reflection," a technique therapists use to mirror back to the patient whatever the patient has told them. The normal procedure involves a reflective statement followed by a mildly interpretive comment or question, such as, "You say that you feel used by your lover [reflection], and yet you continue to see him whenever he calls [comment]." When therapy is going well, this technique is a subtle and effective method of encouraging a patient to think about himself without making him feel defensive. But during a direct confrontation, of course, the technique can be maddening. Your therapist's making statements like "You feel I am trying to hold you in therapy" does not clear anything up, and it can be read as a form of avoidance.

Bill's therapist did not avoid the issue. He went on to ask why Bill had chosen to sit in the chair, and Bill told him. Directly addressing the issue proved successful for Bill. His therapist readily confessed to having performed a "self-analysis" during the intervening week as to why he had made the mistake—a clear admission of error on his part, which mollified Bill considerably. Though his therapist was not willing to say more, he had at least acknowledged playing a role in the contretemps.

Many therapists, once they realize how they are coming across, will alter or drop the tactics you object to. Eventually, Laurie's therapist also proved to be reasonable on this score. For several days after her therapist had told her that her wish to leave indicated her difficulty in committing to relationships "like marriage," Laurie fumed privately, certain now that her therapist was trying to hold her back. Finally anger made her bold: she came to therapy and told him outright that she felt he was trying to intimidate her into staying. Her therapist softened his position at once. He said that what he had meant by "not ready" was simply that she could benefit from *more* therapy, not that she was courting disaster by leaving. He knew she would do well outside therapy, he now told her; he did not see her marriage as being endangered.

He was not willing, however, to admit that he had indeed made a threat, veiled or otherwise, against her marriage. Therapists will not be analyzed, and if you say directly to a therapist, "I find it suspicious that you would compare marriage to therapy," he is not going to agree. While Laurie's therapist did reassure her, he did not take any blame for a power struggle. However, after this episode he did end all obstructionist behavior and became helpful to Laurie in her efforts to leave. His actions spoke louder than words. If your therapist's behavior changes after you have discussed your concerns with him, it is at least a tacit admission of his role in a

power struggle, and the door is open to further progress either in therapy or toward termination.

Of course, things do not always go this well. When you
cannot convince your therapist to alter his attitude or
behavior, you are then faced with having to leave therapy against his will—or at the very least without his
cooperation. In this case, you are going to have to function as your own therapist, since he has effectively ab-
dicated that role as far as the issue of termination goes.

How to go about analyzing yourself? Basically, in
order to steer yourself safely out of a power struggle
you must come to grips with what disturbs you most
about leaving without your therapist's blessing. Here
the experience of others can help.

Patients who have left therapy against their therapist's advice report that one of the main obstacles to
doing so is their need for his or her approval. Everyone
wants to be admired; whatever your acts and beliefs,
you would like others to think you are right and/or
good. You would particularly like to feel you are right
and/or good in the eyes of your therapist because the
process of transference sets him or her up as a stand-in
parent. When he or she withholds approval—or is outright disapproving—of your decision to leave, you face
a real problem. Almost all patients want to be thought
of as "good patients," and leaving against your therapist's wishes can be emotionally tantamount to a fall
from therapeutic grace. Laurie is a patient who was
willing to stay months—even years—beyond the point
at which she wanted to leave in hope of finally winning
her therapist's approval. This is not uncommon.

The only real way to deal with a "fall from grace" is
simply to acknowledge it outright. You want your therapist's approval for leaving; you are not going to *get* his
approval for leaving—and that, as the saying goes, is

that. Consciously instructing yourself to give up trying to win approval can help you leave when you want to. While you may still *wish* for your therapist's blessing, you are no longer *acting* upon this wish. Ultimately emotions catch up with actions. If you take the action of leaving against your therapist's advice, eventually you will come to feel good about it. Time heals.

But what about those patients who *want* to be "bad"? There are those people who pride themselves on being different, people who can stand up for themselves no matter what others think. Paradoxically, such patients may find it even more difficult to walk away from a power struggle.

Marty, a television producer accustomed to holding his own with belligerent Hollywood types, found that his willingness to do battle stymied him every time he tried to quit therapy. "The first time I decided to quit," he recalls, "I went to my session, lay down on the couch, and announced I was leaving." His therapist's response was to sidestep the issue, focusing instead on the manner in which Marty had raised it. Marty, he said, had presented his decision *provocatively;* rather than open a topic for discussion, Marty had issued a challenge. Moreover, his therapist continued, this was characteristic of his dealings with others.

For Marty, this exchange was an unmistakable red flag. He insisted he *hadn't* been provocative; his therapist came back with the observation that Marty seemed bothered by the word *provocative*. Marty replied that he wasn't bothered, and on it went. The hour was intense and unsatisfactory, and Marty spent the days preceding his next session plotting a new line of attack.

In short, Marty was now engaged in battle with his own therapist, and for Marty, nothing was more compelling than a fight. He wanted to win the argument, and of course you cannot hope to win an argument with a therapist, because therapists are trained not to argue. The classic therapist's response to a patient's bid for a quarrel is to remark that the patient seems to feel like quarreling. Marty found himself more locked into therapy than ever. Arguing (or *trying* to argue) with your therapist about leaving therapy is a quite different activity from actually leaving therapy.

The need for meaning is one of the most compelling forces that can hold you in a power struggle with your therapist. Anyone who has chosen to spend many months in therapy has a profound need for insight. You seek to understand, to comprehend, to *know why*, and a power struggle produces only confusion. If you suggest the presence of a power struggle to your therapist and he rejects this possibility, what do you conclude? Your therapist may be trying to exercise power over you, or he may be acting according to what he sees as your best interests, or he may be doing both—and you are probably not going to be able to sort it all out no matter how many clues you spot.

Therapists are purposely vague on most subjects concerning their patients. Generally speaking, they do not make direct analyses. Rather, they try to maneuver their patients delicately toward arriving at these analyses on their own. But when it comes to a power struggle, such indirectness can cause a problem because you are trying to discover a truth not just about *yourself* but about your *therapy* as well. If your therapist hints that you are leaving therapy because you have trouble with open-ended relationships like marriage, is this an accurate analysis, a threat, an observation, or a simple mistake? Is "therapy equals marriage" even what he *means* by the few words he has spoken? Not knowing and *wanting* to know can hold you in therapy long after you are ready to leave.

When you cannot decide what the truth of the matter

is, you must find a way to live with the uncertainty. The best way to do this is to redefine your terms. The real question, ultimately, is not "Am I involved in a power struggle?" It is "Am I ready to leave?"

Forcing yourself to stop analyzing your therapist's motives and to focus purely on your own will be a challenge. Any mystery is compelling, and when you truly cannot comprehend your therapist's behavior, you risk becoming obsessed with the effort to do so. Fixating on therapy is no way to leave therapy, nor is it any way to be in therapy. When you cannot let go of your suspicions, you are implicitly making a decision to stay in therapy but not to fully trust your therapist—the worst of both worlds.

If you truly want to leave, and if your therapist truly is not going to help you leave, then termination is up to you. You must *disengage*. Stop seeking approval, stop seeking arguments, stop seeking clues, stop seeking whatever it is you most hope—or fear—to find. When it becomes clear that your therapist is not going to give you the send-off you desire—*for whatever reason*—you have to do without.

By now, if your therapy has been effective, you should be up to this challenge. And if your therapy has not been effective, it is time to find a therapy that *will* be.

Chapter ELEVEN

BEYOND
THERAPY

Therapy does not end with goodbye. After your final session has come and gone, you are left with a confusion of feelings, questions, lingering concerns. This is true for any therapy, including the most successful. No one leaves therapy with his life wrapped up neatly in one shining package.

It is your task in the weeks and months after therapy to sort out these feelings. The place to start is with the fear you may have of the unknown. Therapy can be so powerful, so all-encompassing, that stepping outside of it feels like venturing into uncharted territory. Even if your therapy has occupied only a small corner of your existence, still you may wonder what giving it up means for your future. What is life going to be like without therapy? Yes, you will be returning to normal life, but it will be normal life *without therapy,* a life entirely on your own.

If you have been seeing a therapist for many months or years, you may not be convinced that life on your own holds much appeal. In the words of one former patient, "My therapist's office always seemed mystical to me. Things happened there." For many patients, therapy supplies an element of magic. In therapy, "things happen" concerning every aspect of your existence, down to the most intimate detail. When it is going well, it can seem as if therapy is—or over time has come to be—the sustaining base of all you cherish. Take away the base and collapse appears imminent.

But as we have seen, after therapy most people's lives hold firm. The reality—as opposed to the frightening fantasy—is that our worlds are far more durable than we might suspect, held together as they are by myriad relationships, habits, and enduring values. Therapy turns out to be only one source of strength among many. Your first discovery in the weeks and months after therapy is that you can, in fact, function very well without therapy.

Your emotions during this period will probably run the gamut. Among the most positive reactions is a sense of exhilaration—a feeling that life is beginning again. Remember Phoebe, who felt "elated" that she had "escaped." It seems fair to assume that she also felt elated because she had just been launched on her new life post-therapy. Most people also experience a sense of real loss during the days and months immediately following therapy. The week after Phoebe terminated, when the hour arrived for her normally scheduled appointment she felt a mixture of sadness and happiness. She was proud of herself for leaving, but sad that she would not be seeing her therapist that afternoon.

In the first days after therapy has ended, some former patients do feel worse. It is not uncommon to go through a kind of mourning, and ex-patients develop various ways of coping. Some hold mental conversations with their therapists for weeks or months after leaving; others have fantasies of reunion, imagining themselves running into their therapist on the street, at a party, in the supermarket. Still other ex-patients maintain some form of contact with their therapists. They send notes, often accompanied by cartoons, clippings, drawings, poems—especially cartoons.

Cartoons serve the purpose well, because a line drawing says so much with so little: a picture is worth a thousand words. Since just after therapy's end you may *want* to say a thousand words (or more) to your therapist, and yet at the same time you refuse to weaken in your resolve to make it on your own, a cartoon is the perfect way to express these conflicting impulses. When you send your therapist a cartoon, you manage to say a great deal all at once, without precisely owning up to how much you (still) want to talk. And, of course, with a cartoon you are no longer "talking" at all; you have moved out of the verbal realm into the visual. Symbolically you are shifting away from the analytic mode so basic to therapy to a kind of shorthand comment, which is a more everyday fashion of dealing with life. And when you condense a thousand words into one picture, you are starting to sum things up for yourself as well—a crucial part of the post-therapy period. In short, a cartoon sent to a therapist is a way of saying "hello" and "goodbye" and "this is how I feel" all at once.

Many ex-patients—much to their therapists' chagrin —cope with their sense of loss by withholding that final check. There are countless cases of former patients who maintain contact with their therapists for *years* either by never quite getting around to sending that last payment or by treating their therapist's final bill like a credit statement and paying it off "over time"—and *more* time. Some therapists, wittingly or not, participate in this ploy. One ex-patient who was still paying off her final bill one year after ending treatment told me that her therapist continued to write and

send cards throughout this period, always expressing
interest in how she was doing. Her strong feeling was
that she would not be hearing from him if she were all
paid up.

But if you are serious about wanting to make it on your
own without therapy, the period of missing your therapist simply has to be gotten through. You leave therapy
and you miss your therapist, but you don't go back.
Perhaps you send the occasional note or card, but you
do not return for sessions.

Fortunately, this exercise of will is necessary only for
the period of time it takes truly to *leave* therapy in your
mind as well as in fact. During this period you do not
need to punish yourself with the thought that being out
of therapy means never, ever seeing your therapist—or
any other therapist—again. A good termination should
not end in absolute loss. Instead, it leaves the former
patient free to return from time to time for what therapists have dubbed a "booster"—one or more quick sessions to deal specifically with some new challenge that
has arisen in the patient's life.

Booster sessions can be extremely productive. One
former patient, a thirty-four-year-old network executive, discovered this when she developed cold feet just
before her marriage. Originally, Corinne had gone into
therapy in her early thirties to deal with issues concerning men and marriage. Never married, she had just
left a long-term live-in lover largely on the grounds
that while stable and reasonably happy, their four-year
relationship was strictly informal. Marriage was not in
the cards.

Newly returned to the Los Angeles dating scene, she
found herself having a very hard time. And she discovered, too, that she was ambivalent at the prospect of
marriage and children and what one might have to do

to take that path. Therapy helped ease her through the "dating wars," and eventually—not long after she had met the man she planned to marry—she terminated. Her leave-taking had all the hallmarks of a coming-of-age: she was, in her mind, making the transition to adult life—marriage, children, responsibility—and she wanted to be out of therapy, on her own. Her therapist readily let her go.

However, as the day of her marriage drew near, Corinne panicked. She was wracked by doubt, so much so that she was on the verge of canceling the elaborate family wedding that had been planned. At this point she returned to her therapist specifically to deal with the crisis.

Her therapist quickly and competently talked Corinne through it. In a handful of sessions he helped her sort out realistic misgivings from sheer, never-been-married panic. Corinne went on to marry her fiancé and have a child. What would have happened if her therapist had not been there for her to turn to is anyone's guess. Perhaps she would have canceled the ceremony; perhaps not. But even if her therapist did not save the wedding, certainly he dramatically resolved the crisis and eased her transition into marriage. And he did so without jolting her back to full-fledged patient status, with all that being a patient implies.

Corinne's experience represents the ideal termination, followed by the ideal post-termination period. She could be helped by her therapist without having to rekindle her "transference neurosis." When Corinne exited therapy her transference neurosis was resolved, while the other half of her therapeutic relationship— the therapeutic alliance—was left intact. This allowed her to *stay* out of therapy long enough really to *be* out; after a couple of months on her own she was no longer a patient in her own mind. And when a crisis arose, she could get help quickly without having to develop, and then work through, an entire transference neurosis once more. She could approach her therapist not as a stand-in mother/father/lover but as an esteemed professional offering essential expertise.

Not all endings go so smoothly. In an unsatisfactory termination the transference remains unresolved, even though the therapy has ended. And when the transference remains, it may spell trouble for your life after therapy. If your supposed ex-therapist never really makes it to the category of "ex," he or she becomes, not your former therapist, but your once and future therapist. You are still in therapy *in your head* even though you are no longer in therapy in fact. You continue to think of your therapist as your Therapist, like an ex-husband who is still mentally married to his ex-wife. You may then find yourself rejecting any future contact whatsoever with him in order to keep yourself from falling back into full-time therapy. Where other ex-patients can return to their therapists for booster sessions, or just to check in and be friendly, you may be forced to maintain an absolute moratorium on relations.

When a terminating patient's transference remains alive, the therapist is, in most cases, at least partially to blame. Some therapists *consistently* leave their patients in a state of unresolved transference, while others consistently do not—which implies that a good termination requires the cooperation of your therapist.

According to Leo Rangell, an analyst who has written extensively about termination, poor terminations are often a result of the therapist's refusal to undo what Rangell terms the "psychoanalytic situation." For the patient, the psychoanalytic situation is the position of being the *patient:* being the needy one, the one who re-

quires help and interpretation. When therapy is ending, the patient must move out of this position into a
normalized relationship with his therapist, *and the
therapist must cooperate in this move.* When the therapist does not, the patient remains a patient to some
degree, with all the dependency that condition implies.

If you have left a therapist who has not allowed the
psychoanalytic situation to shift toward a more normalized relationship, you may find yourself spending
your months and years of post-therapy longing for
more therapy, or actually back in therapy. This is the
fate of more than a few former patients. Bernie Zilbergeld actually goes so far as to say that "One of the most
consistent and important effects of counseling is a desire for more counseling." He offers various studies of
repeat patients to prove the point. One survey of therapy patients *in their early twenties* found that a full 64
percent had been in therapy before. In Zilbergeld's own
practice more than 80 percent of his clients had seen
other therapists before coming to him.

Laurie, the patient whose therapist delayed her termination by nearly two years, encountered one version
of this effort to hold on. As she neared her final session,
her therapist suggested that she might want to return
to therapy one day—specifically, he said, once she had
children. "You might want to talk to a therapist about
any problems you have with your daughter," he added.

At the time, Laurie did not find the suggestion off-
putting. In fact, she felt secretly pleased that her therapist expected her to go on to have children with her
husband, especially given his doubts about her capacity for commitment. And she was happy to hear that in
his view she was destined to have a girl. She wanted a
girl.

His prediction of a daughter in her future also fitted
smoothly with her own perception of herself. She

thought of herself as a woman who would have girl children—and her friends thought of her the same way. Somehow, perhaps because of her strong friendships with other women, she simply *seemed* the kind of woman who would give birth to girls. So at the most benign level, her therapist was simply seeing her as she saw herself—and as the people she cared about saw her, too.

Later Laurie began to perceive these final remarks in another light altogether. For one thing, after all the trouble she had had convincing her therapist to accept her decision to leave, this parting shot read like a last-minute withdrawal of approval. Or perhaps it was a sign that he had never really accepted her termination at all, and he was now trying to soften her disturbing termination-for-good into a nonthreatening termination-for-now. When it became clear that she was indeed leaving *this* therapy, he seemed to be falling back to the position that she would one day return for *another* therapy—with another therapist. Laurie found this irritating.

She also began to bridle at his automatic assumption that she would find having children so difficult that she would inevitably require therapy to cope. This was hardly the vote of confidence with which she would have liked her therapy to end. Here was her therapist projecting major problems with motherhood into her future, sending her off with a vision of trouble lurking on the horizon, and all this in soothing tones of warmth and reassurance. It was a classic mixed message. More, it was very probably a display of countertransference; why else would he take it for granted Laurie would have a girl? His choice of words was "your daughter," not "*if* you have a daughter."

When in real life Laurie gave birth to a boy, the emotional basis of her therapist's recommendations for her future therapy suddenly became clear. Obviously, his feeling that she was destined to become the (troubled) mother of a daughter came from something within his relationship to her, not from any objective capacity to predict her future. And, of course, for a *therapist* to assume that his young, ambitious, and high-strung female patient would one day bear a daughter (with whom she could not get along!) is quite a different matter from that woman's friends and family making a similar assumption. Given his position as her therapist, as one who knew things about her that she herself apparently did not, Laurie ultimately began to feel almost as if he had been trying to "cast a spell" over her future motherhood, making predictions that would stay with her and perhaps become self-fulfilling.

All told, Laurie's final sessions seem to indicate that her therapist was not willing to give up the psychoanalytic situation. While with this issue, as with all others, it is impossible to sort out which party contributes what to a given therapeutic result, clearly some therapists do their part to encourage repeat therapies. In Laurie's case the impetus toward repeat therapy came entirely from her therapist; she herself viewed her leave-taking as final. Having gone into therapy in a state of profound pain, she did not relish the thought that she would again one day feel that bad or that desperate. And she did not appreciate such a future being (implicitly) predicted for her by her therapist.

It is apparent that people do not simply stop therapy; they are not in therapy one day and out the next. There exists a distinct therapy aftermath, a *post-therapy phase*. The most obvious manifestation of this period is the powerful emotions you are likely to experience, ranging from sadness, grief, and regret, to possible disillusionment and anger, to pride and even exhilaration.

Your emotions during this period are likely to be complex and often unpredictable. But the post-therapy phase involves considerably more than just thrashing through a bundle of feelings. Judging by the progress many patients make only after leaving therapy, these weeks and months deserve to be seen as a distinct and important part of therapy—as the actual final stage of a therapy well done.

Ruth's experience shows how the work of therapy completes itself after therapy. When she entered therapy Ruth was a thirty-three-year-old woman who was troubled on all fronts; she was experiencing problems with men, problems at work, problems with self-confidence, problems with a consuming anxiety and concern. By the time she emerged from treatment, she was on her way to marrying a man she had met while in therapy, and she had made real strides at work as well. From her point of view, therapy had been a success.

Even so, Ruth left with certain complaints, which would only be resolved during the post-therapy phase. "My therapy focused mainly on my relationship with my mother," she explains, "which meant that we spent a lot of time tracing everything wrong with my life back to her. My problems with men, my problems with work—in therapy it just seemed as if she was *behind* it all. I used to leave sessions furious with her—even though except for my teenage years we had always gotten along great."

In short, for Ruth therapy was stirring up ancient business, reopening very old wounds. Ruth's father had died young, leaving Ruth's mother to manage on her own. Although the marriage had not been happy, its passing had thrown Ruth's mother into yet worse relationships with men: struggling to support herself and her young daughter, Ruth's mother had had to find work as a secretary—one of the few kinds of employment open to women in the '50s—working for men who were often less educated than she. With no prospects for advancement, no hope that over the years money would ever become less tight for her child and herself, she bitterly resented her male employers' control over her life. And she never remarried.

Faced with this daily struggle, she relayed the message to her daughter that men are the enemy and a woman can't hope to make it in a man's world. Ruth and her therapist were able to trace the roots of Ruth's own troubles with men and work back to this childhood theme. All her life she had heard that relations between the sexes, in love and in work, were hopeless. Small wonder she was so troubled now.

But Ruth's therapy did not stop at this insight. "My therapy spilled over from my head to my mother's head all the time," she explains. "We didn't just analyze *my* motives; we analyzed hers, too. Pretty soon I began to see my mother not as the victim she'd always presented herself as, but as someone who somehow *wanted* to be a victim. And worse—as a mother who wanted her daughter to be just as unhappy as she had been."

One session in particular stands out in Ruth's memory. "We were talking about my first two-wheel bicycle," she remembers. "My mother had saved all year to get it, and the first time I rode it I fell off and twisted my ankle so badly she had to take me to the hospital for X-rays. Then I couldn't walk—or ride—for days. The thing is, when I finished telling that story in therapy—I don't remember now why it came up—my therapist said, 'And how do you feel about that?' And I heard myself saying that I felt like my mother wanted me to fall. That she wanted me to fall then, and fail now."

This was a painful moment for Ruth; she felt enormous guilt for even having such a thought. Her mother had been utterly devoted to her, had sacrificed, worked, and saved to care for her, and here was Ruth at age thirty-three sitting in a therapist's office saying, 'My mother wanted me to fall.' Yet the thought struck her with the force of truth.

From one perspective, Ruth now believes, it was the truth—that is, one facet of the truth. While it is unlikely in the extreme that her mother wanted to see her precious daughter career off a new bike onto a hard cement sidewalk, it probably is the case that her mother feels some ambivalence about the worldly success possible for young women of Ruth's generation, which was denied her in her own youth. It is not that Ruth's mother wants her to fail, but that she wishes the conditions of her own life could have been different. However, Ruth found it impossible, within the confines of therapy, to see things in this sensible light.

To some extent Ruth's inability to do so was due to the very nature of therapy, which deals in *unconscious* —unconsciously *negative*—motives. Within the context of therapy a mother's failings look like more than failings; they look like unconscious acts of aggression: *"My mother wanted me to fall."* In therapy your loved ones often appear worse than they really are because therapy is more than a technique, it is a certain way of seeing people and reality, a worldview. And this worldview is frequently dark. You *look for* negative motives in yourself and in those around you.

Furthermore, most therapists employ a modified free-association approach characterized by the frequently posed question, "How does that make you feel?" And when you are invited to voice the first feelings that come to mind within a Freudian context you can come up with some pretty dark sentiments: *"My mother wanted me to fall."* The trouble is, because therapy validates the "truth value" of feelings (as it should), this sentiment will strike the patient uttering it as absolutely on target, as a *discovery*. Outside therapy, of course, such a sentiment loses much of its power and, perhaps, much of its reality. "My mother wanted me to fall" sounds more real in session than out. This is so because what seems real at any given moment is powerfully influenced by time and place; social reality shifts ground constantly.

A good therapist will be at pains to urge his patient to see that the truth he discovers in sessions is, in fact, the truth of how he *feels*—and not necessarily the truth of how things really are or were. This was certainly the case with Ruth's therapist. "Basically," she says, "I would go to therapy and come back out all riled up at my mother. This would go on session after session. But the thing is, I don't think it was really my therapist's fault. He was constantly steering me back to a more reasoned view. He would say things like 'Don't you think your mother takes pride in your accomplishments?' But somehow, it didn't work. I still felt awful about my mother no matter what he said." For as long as she remained in therapy, Ruth could not achieve a more balanced view of her mother's life and its influence on her.

Her difficulty here stemmed from the fact that in therapy, you go over the minute details of the personal encounters in your life, and you inevitably reawaken all the emotions associated with those details. Moreover, in therapy you often go over *past* details. The problem with focusing upon the past is that even reinterpretation of the past cannot make it look altogether different. Going over the details of painful childhood memories amounts to a double whammy: these details evoke powerful emotions in and of themselves, while reviewing long-past details gives you the feeling that these bad episodes are writ in stone. In memory you

will always fall off the bicycle; you will always *have* to
fall off the bicycle.

The details of your present life and relationships are
quite different in this respect, because they exist in an
ongoing process of being worked out and altered.
Maybe your lover came home late last night without
calling to tell you first. True, this particular detail cannot be changed, but the possibility that he *will* call next
time remains open. In short, yesterday's negative details feel a great deal more fluid—and hence a great
deal less damning—than the details of your childhood,
which is over and done with. In therapy long-past
"sins" may loom much larger than the ones that are
happening around you right now.

In Ruth's case, she found the process of examining
negative scenes from her childllhood particularly painful because she had been very close to her mother, as
one would expect the only daughter of a widowed
mother to be. All her life she had idealized her mother,
and now the sentiments she gave voice to in therapy
were driving a wedge between them. This may have
been necessary; Ruth probably needed to pull away
from her mother in order to establish herself as a separate, grown woman relating to men on her own, not her
mother's, terms. But she did not want independence at
the cost of her deep love and admiration for her only
living parent.

This conflict was resolved in Ruth's post-therapy period. "It wasn't until about two years after I left therapy," she reports, "that everything I'd talked about
there came together." Two years after leaving therapy,
Ruth found herself able to think of her mother in loving
yet more realistic terms. The mother she had adored
since childhood began to merge with the mother she
had been so furious with in therapy, and the resulting
picture was a happy one.

In part, this post-termination clarity resulted from the upward spiral Ruth found herself in as a result of treatment. In the two years after therapy, her life continued to improve. Because there is nothing like happiness to increase your tolerance of others, Ruth had come to feel better about her mother, just as she felt better about everyone—and everything—else in her life. In addition, as her therapy sessions receded in memory, Ruth began to assign credit as well as blame to her mother. "Somehow," she says, "I began to see—to really *feel*—that it wasn't only my problems I got from my mother. It was also my capacity to meet problems head-on; it was most of the things I value in myself. I learned persistence from her, and I learned the importance of hard work and of standing by the people you love. And I learned how to survive."

In light of all Ruth's mother had given her, the bad parts of their relationship began to fade in significance. As Ruth puts it, "I began to see my mother's 'crimes' as mere misdemeanors." This was, of course, the mature attitude her therapist had been urging all along, but it did not set in until the post-therapy period. Ruth feels convinced that, in fact, it could not have taken hold during therapy. She needed time away from dredging up long-lost scenes from her childhood and adolescence in order to put it all together.

Whether they realize it or not, most ex-patients need this time. People need a post-therapy period to assimilate all that has passed in therapy: to make this material their own, apart from the therapeutic session and their therapist's sphere of influence, and to incorporate it into their normal everyday lives. Ruth emerged from a successful therapy into a successful *post*-therapy. Both were essential.

During her post-therapy period Ruth also noticed another process. The countless insights concerning her mother and herself that she had had in therapy coalesced into one central perception. As she describes it, "Over time I began to see that my mother *had* been terrific *as a mother,* which is what I had always thought before I went into therapy. But *as a person* she went through a lot of unhappiness—a bad marriage, early widowhood, low-paying woman's work. It was her personal problems, not her mothering, that affected me badly. Just from living with her I learned to be upset about the same things she was upset about." This insight about her mother—good as a parent, struggling as a human being—had in fact come up in therapy, but again it had not really registered. The time period after therapy allowed this particular insight to emerge as the central perception among the countless other insights she had had, both large and small.

Essentially, what occurs in the post-therapy period is a cognitive sorting process. In traditional therapy the sheer number of interpretations a patient must keep track of can be overwhelming, and they all may seem equally valid and equally significant at the time they surface in therapy. The post-therapy period allows a crucial "forgetting" to occur. During this period lesser ideas and perceptions slip away, while the truly profound insights remain.

The same cognitive process goes on when people speak of gaining "distance" or "perspective" on their problems. Gaining distance is crucial to *understanding,* to how you end up explaining your problems to yourself. Distance in this cognitive sense means that the welter of detail that can overwhelm you in the time of your difficulties begins to fall away. A "big picture," a *theme,* emerges almost unbidden.

This theme is essential to solving your problems and living your life. Now thirty-five and in a happy relationship, Ruth had to decide at last whether she wanted children. Because that decision is saturated with one's feelings and perceptions of one's own parents, Ruth needed a clear picture of *who her mother was* in order to reach her own decision. If her mother-image had remained overly complex and confused, had she continued to feel as angry toward her mother as she had when she left therapy, her thoughts about whether she herself was destined for motherhood might have remained overly complex and confused as well.

Ultimately therapy helped her make a decision to start a family, but she needed the post-therapy period in order to sort out her feelings and arrive at this conclusion. She needed the *clarity* that comes with distance and perspective. With that clarity she could move on to have children of her own, confident that she would be able to give them all her mother had given her, while avoiding her mother's mistakes, if mistakes they were.

At the same time, she could also now accept the real possibility that she *might* in fact repeat the elements of her mother's pattern that had brought her finally to therapy. As a new mother herself, Ruth could try to be the best mother possible, as her own mother had, but she could not promise her unborn children that she would lead a blissfully contented life for the rest of her days. Perhaps a mother's personal problems inevitably took a toll on her children, Ruth now thought; perhaps her own children would grow up anxious about her problems in the same way she had grown up anxious about her mother's. If so, she could forgive herself this in advance. No longer angry with the mother of her childhood, as she had been in therapy, she no longer needed to reject motherhood itself.

In short, Ruth, in leaving therapy, was growing up, taking the responsibility for her adult life—and for whatever mistakes she might make in that life—that her therapist had encouraged her to take. She was reaching the point at which she would no longer blame her mother for her problems (though she could see the connecting lines between the two), at which she would no longer depend on her therapist to side with her against her mother (though she was grateful for his past support), at which she would no longer be angry and confused. Over the course of a successful therapy she had worked through her feelings toward her mother, toward men, toward motherhood. And now, two years after her therapy, she had assimilated the insights that had emerged from that working-through; she was ready to embrace the next phase of her life. And that is the happy end point of a therapy well done: the confidence to move forward, to *act*. To make decisions, to act on those decisions, and to accept the consequences both good and bad; to lead a strong and clear-sighted existence in the face of life's complexities.

The process of termination is essential to reaching this point. Being encouraged by your therapist, as part of an ongoing therapy, to stand on your own is finally not the same thing as simply standing on your own. No matter how adamantly your therapist insists that you take responsibility for your life, the very fact that someone else is nudging you to do so limits how full that responsibility will be. Intrinsically, the therapy setup puts the therapist in a parental position. And it puts you, the patient, in the position of the child. You may become a very wise and grown-up child, but a grown-up child is a different breed from a grown-up pure and simple.

And that is the goal in leaving therapy: to become a grown-up pure and simple. Becoming a grown-up means making peace with the grown-ups you have known and loved, or hated and rebelled against; making peace, or at least coming to terms, with your real parents. A *completed* therapy can help you reach this peace.

And therapy reaches completion only when you set completion as a goal. No therapist can conclude your therapy for you; he can only see you through. It is up to you to understand that it is time to move on, that you are ready to go. That you have done what you came to do. To grow and change and learn through therapy, you must commit yourself to being in therapy, and you must commit yourself to being back out of therapy one day. You must see it through all the way, from start to middle to end and on through postscript: on to the time when, as Freud wrote so movingly half a century ago, you are ready to reach out and claim the right to your own share in life.

ACKNOWLEDGMENTS

I did not come to the subject of leaving therapy by chance. I would never have written this book if I had not been in therapy myself; if I had not myself faced the difficult and sometimes saddening task of finishing therapy with a therapist who had helped me turn my life around. Thus I owe my first and most fundamental debt of gratitude to my own therapist of some years back, Dr. James Sparing. I thank him here for his insight, his caring, and his always warm sense of humor. It was Dr. Sparing who helped me find my way to the upward spiral that is therapy's true happy ending.

Beyond what I learned from Dr. Sparing, I gained much from talks with many other practicing therapists, among them Marilyn Ruman, Sonya Rhodes, Joseph P. Aguayo, Joan Rosenblatt, and Margaret Smith. Peter Loewenberg and Fredrick Redlich also generously shared their own work on the subject.

I have drawn extensively upon the work of several theorists and researchers: Robert S. Wallerstein, Hans H. Strupp and Jeffrey L. Binder, Arnold Z. Pfeffer, Leo

Rangell, Stephen K. Firestein, Bernie Zilbergeld, and
—obviously—the works of Sigmund Freud. To all of
them I owe a great deal.

I would like also to thank my editors at *Self* and *New
Woman*, Caryl Avery and Donna Jackson, who stole
time from frantic schedules to discuss the issue of termination—and who have taught me more than I can
say about their readers and the issues and problems
they face. Because of my association with Caryl and
Donna, I see life differently today.

My editors at Simon and Schuster, Fred Hills, his assistant Jenny Cox, and Burton Beals, were terrific.
They consistently knew exactly what I was trying to do
in each chapter, and consistently came up with ways to
do it better. In particular, Jenny Cox's lucid and compelling editorial letter set me a steady course through
the process of revision.

I would also like to thank Elaine Markson for first
recognizing the potential book in leaving therapy, and
as always I owe much to her associate, my agent Geri
Thoma: it was she who came up with the guiding
maxim of the work, "You need therapy for leaving therapy."

Closest to the heart are my family and friends. While
none of them was in therapy during the time I was
writing the book, all were willing to talk about therapy
at length whenever I brought the subject up—and to
cheer me on whenever I didn't. As I embarked upon the
second draft of the book Anette Sikjaer arrived to care
for our baby, Jimmy, bringing with her warmth and
life, setting just the tone one needs in one's household
when struggling to revise. And finally, to my husband,
Ed, I owe everything; he has brought me love, romance, intellectual and creative exchange. This book is
dedicated to him and to my parents.

I have saved for last those people who shared their own stories of leaving therapy with me. With great generosity they recounted their experiences, both good and bad. This book is about them, and for them.